Time to Stand and Stare

Facing page: sketch of Davies by Powys Evans, 1922

Barbara Hooper

Time to Stand and Stare

A Life of W.H. Davies, the Tramp-Poet

PETER OWEN PUBLISHERS

London and Chester Springs

PETER OWEN PUBLISHERS
73 Kenway Road, London SW5 0RE

Peter Owen books are distributed in the USA by
Dufour Editions, Inc., Chester Springs, PA 19425-0007

First published in Great Britain 2004
© Barbara Hooper 2004

ISBN 0 7206 1205 5

A catalogue record for this book is available from the British Library

Printed and bound in India by
Thomson Press Ltd

To Anne, Isobel, Joanna and Pam

Acknowledgements

I am especially grateful for their help and encouragement to W.H. Davies's great-nephew, Norman Phillips, who showed me around Glendower, as well as lending me family photographs and recordings, and to Davies's heir, Peter Flavell, who showed me his unique collection of Davies first editions. These two provided information and assistance I could not have gleaned from any other source. Among those who once knew him, and provided unique insights, I must mention Myfanwy Thomas, daughter of Edward Thomas, Zena Powell of Newport, Elsie Sparrow of Nailsworth and Peggy Drake of Stratford-upon-Avon. All were in or approaching their nineties when I got in touch with them.

Jim Riches of Lydney kindly showed me his private collection of Davies manuscripts and memorabilia, built up over many years, and Ben Stone and Molly Wheeler of the Harry Ransom Humanities Research Center at the University of Texas helped me to access information from the university's archive of Davies books. For information about Davies's journeyings in North America I am indebted to Professor John Macksey of Baltimore, Sandy Buttle at the Victoria Hospital, Renfrew, and Carol McCuaig, also of Renfrew, author of the Victoria Hospital centenary volume.

In England I have had contact with Sylvia Harlow, whose bibliography of W.H. Davies has been invaluable; with Professor Brian Locke, who put me in touch with Baltimore friends; with George Turner, a legal colleague of Davies's solicitors, the Haines family – his firm are the Davies literary executors; and with Jessica Douglas Home, biographer of Violet Gordon Woodhouse. I have also consulted librarians at Reading University and the University of Wales.

The staff of several public libraries have been extremely helpful, in particular those of Cardiff, Gloucester, Newport, Nailsworth, Stroud and Sevenoaks, as have the staff of the National Portrait Gallery and the Industrial History section of the National Museums and Galleries of Wales. Similarly I owe thanks to the curator of Newport Art Gallery, who allowed me to photograph the Epstein bronze, and I must thank Sheila Weaver for guiding me to the Augustus John collection in the National Museum of Wales. Events in Nailsworth have drawn my attention to aspects of Davies's life in Nailsworth, and I have enjoyed exploring areas of both Newport and

Nailsworth where he lived. Others who have helped me with photographic and picture research or material include Rachel Sedgwick of the Church House Inn at Newport; Jeff Goundrill, a deputy governor at Leyhill Open Prison; Michael Flavell, Eunice Flavell, Matthew Page, Peter Bennett, Emma Butterfield, Margot Clark, Rosemary Walton, Bernard Horrocks and Neil Hudd.

Everyone at Peter Owen has been unfailingly helpful but none more so than my editor Antonia Owen.

Finally I am grateful to my family for encouraging me not to give up.

Foreword

This is the story of a Victorian boy from the Welsh docks who rose to become a London literary celebrity and who, fifty years after his death, had one of his poems voted fourteenth in a poll of the British nation's favourites. Since then millions have heard the poem 'Leisure' on British television advertisements for a chain of leisure centres. But how many of them could have named William Henry Davies as the author or known anything of his extraordinary life?

The poet himself told parts of his own story in *The Autobiography of a Super-Tramp*, chronicling his delinquent Welsh boyhood, his years as a hobo roaming North America until he lost a leg trying to jump a train in Canada and his penniless years writing verse in London doss-houses – until in middle age he emerged as a successful poet, novelist and essayist. But he wrote only fragments about his later life in his prolific output, although he gave tantalizing glimpses of his unusual marriage and his climb to respectability, befriended by such literary giants as George Bernard Shaw, John Masefield, D.H. Lawrence, Joseph Conrad, Rupert Brooke and fellow Welshman Edward Thomas. Throughout his life he seldom settled anywhere for long until he and his wife Helen, half his age, found their dream home in a small Gloucestershire town.

He was painted or sculpted by a dozen famous artists, among them Epstein and Augustus John, and he carved out a new career for himself reading his poems on radio. The story of his marriage to a prostitute came to light in an autobiographical novel published years after his death – its appearance delayed until his wife died. At the time of publication the novel, *Young Emma*, caused something of a literary furore with its revelations.

Davies died childless in 1940, and Helen, herself something of a mystery figure, was to outlive him by forty years. Their seventeenth-century cottage is home now to a great-nephew, Norman Phillips, who has lived there for twenty years. Mysteriously, early editions of Davies's books, his copyright and royalties were left in Helen's will to the grandson of a local chemist who supplied prescriptions for the Davieses.

The poem that won Davies immortality, one of more than seven hundred he wrote in his lifetime, is deceptively simple yet strikes a chord in every listener. Many anthologies have included 'Leisure' since its first publication in 1911, yet it was to be ninety years before television most unexpectedly inspired its renaissance.

Contents

Illustrations between pp. 96 and 97

Victorian Newport, *c.* 1893

The ferryboat *The Welsh Prince,* on which Davies sailed as a boy with his grandfather

The Church House Inn, Newport, where Davies was born

Photo of Davies *c.* 1908, at time of publication of *The Autobiography of a Super-Tramp*

Bronze head of Davies by Jacob Epstein, 1916

Painting of Davies by Augustus John, 1918

No. 14 Great Russell Street, Bloomsbury, where Davies lived from 1916 to 1921

Manuscript of unpublished poem by Davies, *c.* 1921

Painting of Davies by Sir William Nicholson, 1924

Davies in Stonehouse, Gloucestershire, *c.* 1930

Davies and his wife Helen in Stonehouse and Yewdales, Gloucestershire, *c.* 1932

Davies in the doorway of Yewdales in Nailsworth, 1936

Glendower, Nailsworth, where Davies lived from 1937 until his death in 1940

Davies with his nephew in Nailsworth, *c.* 1936

Davies, Helen and John Masefield at the unveiling of the Church House Inn plaque in 1937

The Wixey family, who supplied prescriptions to Davies and his wife in the 1930s

Peter Flavell, Davies's heir and grandson of Louis Wixey, who was aged about six when Davies's will was made *c.* 1940

The prisoners' gold-medal-winning garden at Chelsea Flower Show, 2003, illustrating the poem 'Leisure'

What is this life, if, full of care,
We have no time to stand and stare?

. . .

No time to turn at Beauty's glance
And watch her feet, how they can dance.

– 'Leisure', 1911

So, seeing that my life has been just as wonderful since I became known as an author as it was before, I will now make an attempt to impart some of that wonder to others . . . introducing some of the immortals of Vagrancy to the immortals of Literature and Art whom I have met in my later days.

– *Later Days*, 1925

Victorian Newport and Nailsworth

And well they love to stand and hear
The old seafaring men that fear
Land more than water; carts and trains
More than wild waves and hurricanes.
And they will walk with love and pride
The tattooed mariner beside.

– 'The Call of the Sea'

As far as the poet-tramp William Henry Davies belonged anywhere in his life, he belonged to Newport and to Nailsworth, the towns where he was born and where he died. These were two predominantly Victorian towns almost facing each other across the Severn estuary: one a Welsh seaport near the great South Wales coalfields, the other a small market town centred on wool mills straggling along narrow Cotswold valleys. In the 1870s they were sixty miles apart by road. Newly constructed railways linked them both by way of Bristol; still, like the old joke about the Great Western Railway, a Great Way Round. By the year 2000 the distance had been halved by the building of two huge bridges across the estuary.

In late Victorian times the rail journey was a tedious one through Chepstow, Bristol and Gloucester. This was the route taken by Lydia Davies when she took her three grandchildren from Newport to stay with an aunt in Gloucestershire. One of them would become a famous Anglo-Welsh poet and author. The children had grown up near the docks in Newport, a busy town built hard by the site of a Roman fortress, on the estuary of the river Usk, and growing fast in the industrial age. In the factory-growth years of the late nineteenth century its population rose to 30,000. Until 1830 it was part of the English county of Monmouthshire, but many of its people spoke Welsh and had Welsh ancestors. Nowadays it belongs to Welsh Gwent. Through the nineteenth century men flocked there to work as seamen, dockers, railwaymen, steelworkers, builders; and their families congregated in the redbrick terraced houses of narrow streets leading up from the docks towards the handsome civic centre with its Corn

Exchange, Westgate Hotel, town hall and, from the 1880s on, a Woolworth Store.[1]

Nailsworth, on a much smaller scale, was industrialized too; it produced wool. A population of about 15,000 was served by 112 tradesmen, fifteen of them pub landlords. Quakerism had come to the town in 1655; a Friends' Meeting House was built soon after this, and the town became something of a centre for Nonconformism. Lying on the main road between two spas, Bath and Cheltenham, it was a staging post for Victorian tourists; and a number of handsome villas appeared among the seventeenth-century weavers' cottages and eighteenth-century millworkers' homes. It lay at the western edge of the Cotswolds, and a cluster of woollen mills sprang up where pure water trickled down from the hills. The railway came to Nailsworth – on a branch line from Stonehouse – not long after Isambard Kingdom Brunel's track burrowed its way under the Severn from Bristol towards Newport.

Nailsworth prospered in the 1870s, just as Newport did, from an upsurge of small shops, and new churches, a free library, a mechanics' institute and, within a decade, national schools. Shops multiplied around Nailsworth marketplace. Mill wagons carrying bales of lower-grade cloth (known as 'flock' and 'shoddy') rumbled through on their way to Bristol or the Thames–Severn Canal. Another major place of work was the bacon-curing factory, and production of leatherboard, an imitation of leather, also provided a good many jobs.

At first glance Newport and Nailsworth would seem to have little in common. But Newport was the birthplace and childhood home of that Anglo-Welsh poet, Lydia Davies's younger grandson, and Nailsworth his last home, where he died.

William Henry Davies was born in the Church House Inn in Portland Street, Newport, or at least very close to it, in 1871, and there he grew up. He lived in Nailsworth as a middle-aged married man for twelve years, his longest settled stay anywhere except as a boy. For a man who had spent a quarter of his life roaming England and the USA, begging, sleeping rough, dossing in workhouses, hawking pins and lace, Nailsworth was as much a home as his childhood base at Castell Newydd, the Welsh name for Newport.

The Church House Inn, square and cream-painted, stood – and

still stands – at a road junction not far from the heart of dockland, in an area called Pillgwenlly or Pill. The Celtic origin of the name suggests a marsh by a river or creek, and the Roman town of Caerwent sprang up by the river Usk. Key roads running through Pill's network of terraces were Commercial Street and Commercial Road; Portland Street, named after a Victorian worthy, led off Commercial Road. Pill was a hive of commercial activity in the 1870s with scores of shops and several street markets. A fish, game and fruit merchant had a hundred kinds of fish and fowl temptingly displayed outside his store. A dealer suggestively called Wheeler sold prams, bicycles and babies' bassinettes. The Tredegar District Laundry (run by W. Davies, no relation) proclaimed that it laundered dress shirts. Around the corner from Portland Street was a fishmonger named Flook; another Davies hired out bicycles, sold flowers and gramophone records; a fruiterer delivered from a decorated banana cart.

Pill streets clanged with the sound of horses' hooves and the strident bells of horse-drawn trams (electric trams were still thirty years away). When Davies was a boy a twenty-seater Corporation bus, its open upper deck reached by outside steps, ran four times a day down Commercial Street to the docks. Horse-drawn charabancs took locals on works outings to Barry Island. Pill was a poor area. A dilapidated poorhouse in 1840 gave way to a grander workhouse, and the poorhouse was converted to a national school. Pill had three police houses and an extraordinary number of rag-and-bone merchants. By 1870 Commercial Road had acquired a few gas lights but no sewage system or pavements. The district had a free library, an infirmary and a range of schools.

Even busier and noisier was the Alexandra Dock, opened in 1868. Shipbuilding was a major industry, and coal, timber and grain were the chief cargoes going through the docks. Freighters under sail, soon succeeded by steamships, crossed the Atlantic to and from Newport. Major repairs went on day and night in the dry dock. Ferries arrived from around the Welsh coast and across the Bristol Channel. Engineering sites, brickworks, india rubber and textile factories mushroomed. This was the age of heavy industrial expansion in South Wales, and the port of Newport was an outlet to the world.

The dock area was awash with pubs, Church House Inn being one of the most popular – a natural landfall for a sailor when he left the sea, providing both home and income for him. William Davies, a Cornish seaman, took over as its landlord when he gave up the sea in the 1860s, bringing with him his wife Lydia and his son Francis, an iron moulder. He chose Newport because his wife was a Newport woman, and it was the northern terminus of a ferry service from Bristol that he had sailed on towards the end of his time at sea. It is not hard to imagine an old salt exchanging yarns over the bar with fellow seamen, tramping the neighbourhood, hanging round the harbour with a telescope watching the movements of ships. William Henry left a poet's sketch of his grandfather, irascible but kind-hearted, gregarious and obsessed with the weather.[2]

Lydia Davies, née Brodribb, came from a talented Anglo-Welsh family with its roots in Somerset. A cousin, John Henry Brodribb, became known to Victorian theatregoers as the actor-manager Sir Henry Irving, and others among her relatives were professional musicians. The Brodribbs were of yeoman stock, originating from Clutton, near Bristol, and Keinton Mandeville in Somerset, with a Cornish branch. John Henry Brodribb was born in a farmhouse at Keinton Mandeville, which is now a pilgrimage place for theatre-history lovers, and Lydia Davies's parents came from the same area.

Early on Brodribb took the stage name Henry Irving and appeared on stage in Sunderland when he was eighteen. His first notable role was in a melodrama, *The Bells*, and he is credited with inventing modern stage lighting. All through his stage career Irving's company presented *The Bells* and *Macbeth*. By 1878 he was managing the Lyceum Theatre in London, playing major Shakespearian roles, touring in the USA and becoming the first British actor to be knighted. At the Lyceum Irving's manager was Bram Stoker, of Dracula fame.[3] Although Davies was in London struggling to get his poems published between 1899 and 1905 – the year of Sir Henry Irving's death – there is no evidence that they ever met. But Davies, a passionate theatre-lover, often stood in the audience for a few pence at the back of West End theatres, and it is easy to imagine that at least once he applauded his celebrated kinsman.

Brodribbs were therefore the maternal ancestors of Davies the poet. Some who knew him later said his features markedly resembled

Irving's, strong and Latinate. The family Spanish look may have owed something to seafaring ancestors with links to both Spain and Cornwall. So Davies's background was far from poverty-stricken, as some writers have suggested, and his ancestry not without artistic talent. The family where he spent his boyhood had a maidservant and a menagerie of pets, including that classic sailor's companion, a parrot.

Davies's ailing father, Francis, disappointed his parents: iron-moulding was an undistinguished occupation, not bringing in much money. He was married young to Mary Ann Evans, a Newport woman and seamstress (she made sails, shirts and overalls) three years older than himself. She was the daughter of Gomer Evans, a boot-maker, and his wife Ann. Francis and Mary Ann had three children: Francis junior, William Henry and Matilda. Francis senior died of tuberculosis, as did many of his contemporaries, in 1874, the same year that his daughter Matilda was born, when William was three and his older brother five.

Davies noted in his *Autobiography* that he was born on 20 April 1871 at the Church House Inn, Newport, but his birth certificate records his birth as occurring on 23 July at 6 Portland Street, two buildings away and long since demolished. He can be forgiven a little artistic licence; his version of events was not always strictly accurate. Probably the Davies grandchildren were indeed born just down the road – two houses and a general store called Mahony's intervened between the inn and number six, the home of Huw Evans who was apparently Mary Ann's brother. In fact the brothers and sister spent most of their early years at the Church House, and Davies may have persuaded himself he was born in April, a month that figured strongly in his adult poems: the month of rainbows, lambs and cuckoos.

Mary Ann was widowed at thirty-four, with no means of support. She did the obvious thing and remarried (her new husband was Joseph Hill), leaving her small children with her parents-in-law. They were shocked but unhesitatingly took on the responsibility. So Francis Boase, a boy who today would be described as having special needs (he had apparently been brain-damaged at birth), William Henry, a toddler, and the baby Matilda were taken in at the Church House Inn by their grandparents and brought up more or less as their own children. In spite of its disadvantages Davies was to remember it as a warm and happy childhood: 'When granny, I, a sister, brother / Huddled under cosy cover'.

He could scarcely remember his father's features, hardly surprisingly since he was three when his father died, and wrote of him only once in his hundreds of verses: under the letter 'R for Remembrance' in his *Poet's Alphabet*:

> All I remember is a coat of velvet, buttoned on his breast,
> Where I, when tired of fingering it, would lay my childish head to rest.[4]

He regretted that he could not recall whether his father was fair or dark, bearded or clean-shaven. Apparently his mother did not often speak of him.

But all through his life he kept a warm affection for his grandfather, the old sea captain ('I am William Davies, master of my own ship!'). The boy spent much time hanging around the harbour, listening to travellers' tales; fairly often his grandfather took him as a treat on board the Newport to Bristol ferry, *The Welsh Prince*, whose captain was a friend. Photographs from the 1880s show her as a chunky vessel with sails and a steam funnel, carrying several dozen passengers sitting above deck and below, as well as a cargo of barrels. Even then she was well equipped with lifeboats and lifebelts. Much of the old man's time was spent on the bridge or in the saloon, but in emergencies he would lend a hand. Davies records a crossing so rough that the ship 'often threatened to dive into the bowels of the deep for peace'. On that occasion Captain Davies was hailed as a hero by other passengers. *The Welsh Prince*, much loved by Newport people, sailed daily as a passenger ship for some fifty years, then as a tug for her last five years at sea, towards the end of the century.

Davies referred later in life to his boyhood as an 'unruly exciting time'. His affection for his grandfather never wavered, as his first published poem as an adult, 'The Soul's Destroyer', indicates:

> I saw sweet treasures of the main,
> Dried fishes, model ships and shells,
> And coral stalks, and seaweed bells,
> In my grandfather's house. Ah! Sweet

To bear his boast through school and street –
'Master of my own ship was I.'
Again I heard his footsteps nigh,
As to and fro the passage dark
He walked, as though on his own bark.

Although the Church House Inn and his early years there figure largely in his autobiography and several of his poems, William's time there ended when he was eight. Captain Davies retired as a licensee and moved with his extended family to Raglan Street and then to Upper Lewis Street. By his teens Davies had developed a fondness for alcohol, mentioned in various poems. By the time he left school he was a fairly heavy drinker, excusing his weakness on the grounds that he had grown up in a pub.

Elsewhere he wrote of his grandfather's kindness to beggars – he 'sternly called them back to give them help'. So began another lifelong interest – in the world of begging; although the schoolboy could hardly have foreseen that he would spend fifteen years of his life on the roads of England, Wales, Canada and the USA as a penniless tramp. The same poem, 'The Child and the Mariner', recalled ships' charts marked with black dots for islands where he imagined 'turtles and palms, and pirates' buried gold'.[5] And another sailor, his great-uncle Henry, loud-voiced and battered of face, evoked mysterious overseas places – Cape Horn, the Caribbean. Henry had a schooner tattooed on his chest but went back to sea only when he had spent all his pay on beer. ('A damn bad sailor and a landshark too . . . My granddad said.')

Anecdotes about his grandfather enliven several of the adult Davies's writings. When the older brother, Francis, was rebuked for some folly Captain Davies had shouted: 'To think he did not have sense enough to shout "Ship ahoy!"' William Henry offered some excuse for Francis: 'The old man paused thunderstruck. "Avast there," he cried "Drop anchor. Will ye have more pudding?"'

Davies as a boy must have met many seamen with strange tales to tell which fed his imagination, some characters even more colourful than his great-uncle Henry, tattooed, gnarled and weatherbeaten. These dockland story-tellers of many nationalities spun their yarns to audiences of fascinated small boys in return for pennies for beer. They saw ships of all kinds docking in the Alexandra Dock, loading and unloading, their global crews coming ashore to search out drink and women. The seafaring tradition went back five hundred years, for in the twenty-first century Pill has made headlines with the archaeological discovery of a medieval wooden boat preserved waterlogged in the marshes of the Usk – the same area where the *The Welsh Prince* ended her seagoing days.

Victorian Newport was an attractive place for an adventurous boy but hardly exciting enough to contain the teenage Davies for long. The sea was in his blood and restlessness in his character.

He was sent to Temple Street Boys' School, just off Commercial Street, and then to Alexandra Road Boys' School, a fairly imposing building offering elementary education up to the age of thirteen. Lawrence Hockey, a Newport man and retired teacher of a later generation (he was born in 1904), researched Davies's childhood and found that at Alexandra Road there was a sound grounding in literature, including English poets such as Thomas Gray.[6] So later critics who suggested Davies had little or no formal education were wide of the mark.

At school Davies discovered a gang composed of juvenile delinquents, truants and shoplifters. This he was happy to join. A Commission of Inquiry set up some years earlier to report on Welsh schools had said of Newport National School's headmaster (not Davies's headmaster): 'He was unable to cope with the ruffian class of children who seemed to come and go as they pleased, learned next to nothing . . . chalked all over the doors and fell into scuffles whenever the master's back was turned.' Newport boys were tough.

Davies wrote relatively little about his schooldays, but occasional references seem to confirm that regard for discipline was not high on his agenda. Hockey reports that the Alexandra Road headmaster, William Richards, was an enlightened teacher with a love of the Bible and also of using the cane. Some of Davies's later prose suggests a biblical influence. His next headmaster was Richard Lewis, the author of a collection of translated Welsh verse (*Cambrian Lyrics*) used as a school textbook. He encouraged in William Henry a love of poetry, so that he became a voracious reader and did well in composition classes. Tennyson, Byron and Shelley featured on his reading lists. He found examinations easy, and he might have gone on to night classes or more advanced education but for his waywardness. According to Hockey he early developed the habit of truanting from school and, worse in Welsh chapel eyes, from Sunday School; spending on food and drink the money intended for the collection plate.

Sport appealed more to him. Although he was unusually short – some said barely over five feet – he excelled at the two traditional Welsh sporting activities of boxing and rugby, and they both feature in his writing. His boxing prowess was encouraged by his maternal grandfather, Gomer Evans.

His lack of height was compensated for by unusual energy and a strong physique, later to be extremely useful to him as an adult. So Davies found himself the leader of a tough and lively gang of boys, who took up shoplifting for greater thrills. In his case the motivation was a genuine love of risk and adventure rather than inherent lawlessness. His *Autobiography* describes how he and five other boys developed a highly successful line in innocent inquiries about prices to obscure their skilful pocketing of small items. 'My girl, Maggie . . . was now the happy possessor of valuable presents in the shape of purses, pocket-books, bottles of scents, pencils of silver.'

All this came to a sudden end when Davies and a fellow thief dropped a bottle of scent, panicked and fled from the shop pursued by witnesses. The boys were kept in a prison cell while detectives searched their homes for stolen goods and Maggie handed over some of her acquisitions. The offences of the five were reported in the local paper, the *Monmouthshire Merlin and South Wales Advertiser*.[7] Despite an offer from Captain Davies to pay a substantial fine, the ringleaders were sentenced to twelve strokes of the birch and the other members of the gang to six. Davies records neither remorse nor distress. From their schoolmaster came a fatherly rebuke which caused the boys more pain than the flogging. Severe grandparental displeasure was an even greater punishment.

It was not the first time that he had been in trouble with his grandmother. In *The True Traveller,* a collection of essays published when he was forty, he tells the tale of a tramp who lived largely by picking up dropped valuables in public parks.[8] This reminds Davies of an escapade when he was a very small boy and had found in the street a ragged handkerchief knotted around some white and yellow coins. His grandmother's fury when he showed them to her puzzled him. Without explanation she gave him a penny and threatened him with drastic punishment if he ever told anyone about his find. The question arises: was Lydia Davies unwittingly setting him on the road to shoplifting and other misdemeanours by not telling the boy that helping himself to crowns and guineas was wrong? His escapades may have stood him in good stead when later he came to live by his wits, and he indicates no remorse for his juvenile delinquency. However, his later verse suggests a strong personal moral streak. As he travelled the world he outgrew his early taste for pilfering, although not entirely for deception; but he would never deceive children, the vulnerable or the very old.

His grandfather was the man of action – 'a straightforward, honest, simple man, with a mortal dread of being in debt' – and his grandmother the moralist of the family. She regularly attended the Commercial Road Baptist Chapel and was imbued with strong puritanical beliefs. As a girl she had been punished for reading a work of fiction; her favourite motto, said her grandson, was 'Procrastination is the thief of time'.

'This ended my schooldays,' Davies wrote laconically of the shoplifting episode. For a while he stayed under unofficial house arrest, beneath the strict eye of his grandparents. He spent the time educating himself by reading and painting ('of course I began with the common penny novel of the worst type, but acquired a taste for better work'). Elsewhere he admits that his 'blood and thunder age, when I read about highwaymen, Indians and scouts, came later, when I was a young man'. The only romantic poet mentioned by name in the boy's reading at this time is Keats, whose lyrical approach to nature influenced Davies as a poet. In his post-school and pre-work period he claims to have read Marlowe, Tennyson and Shakespeare and paid a secret visit or two to Newport's Lyceum Theatre or the Empire – disapproved of by his Baptist grandmother. Another popular entertainment venue was the Assembly Rooms, where Charles Dickens had given one of his famous readings a year before Davies was born. This early love of the theatre led him to try his hand at writing poems and compositions.

When he was not quite fifteen he had a poem about a storm published in the *Monmouthshire Merlin*.[9] His own comment was that 'it lacked rhythm and harmony'. In *The True Traveller*, written many years later, he allowed a brief glimpse into his early ambition to be a writer: 'My first love was painting, and my subjects were ships . . . At that time I was between 13 and 14 years of age . . . one day a boy friend of mine began to tell me about Byron, whose work he was reading. I borrowed the copy at once and from the reading of that book to the present day I have never lost my enthusiasm for poetry.' This inspired him to become a public library addict and to start writing verse.

Perhaps it was in spring cleaning that my own first MS. was lost to the world for ever. I was fourteen years of age at the time, and had taken days and days in going through a dictionary to find three- and four-syllable words for a poem on death: obdurate, invincible, implacable, and many others of that kind . . . That poem was hardly finished before it disappeared, and I told my family that they would know some day what they had done. For several days I was like a little devil, shouting fiercely to the maidservant 'Have you found it?' At last my grandfather, who was an old sea-captain, hearing this question so often, roared in a voice that rattled the cups and saucers, 'Avast there, you aggravating young lubber! Have you lost a schooner of six hundred tons?' Making a dart for the door, I retorted 'Damn you all!' Saying this I gave the door a savage kick and ran into the street. I shall never forget the terrific roar that followed.[10]

He modifies this by saying that his grandfather was a man of passionate storms which quickly blew over; in a moment he would be his good-natured self again, forgetting 'my mutiny'. The episode tells us as much about the teenage Davies as about Captain Davies. In the same volume Davies, not usually a misogynist, indicates his low opinion of women as appreciators of books: 'Very few women have any reverence for a book. They bang a book about without thinking that it contains a human mind. I cannot imagine a woman having any love for books after they are once read. She gives the books away, or lends them without caring if they are returned – she forgets who she has lent them to.'

Lawrence Hockey, interviewed on the radio some years after William's death, said: 'He was always a bit of a daredevil, into boozing and whoring even when he was a lad.'[11] Certainly drink and women featured largely in his adult life.

Another Newport personality who knew Davies locally was his second cousin Zena Powell, born in 1911, who became a professional pianist and artist. Her son Julian asked her when she was ninety if she had any anecdotes about Davies. She recalled her grandmother scolding him: 'When are you going to do some real work?' His reaction was not noted. And on a return visit to Newport Davies, meeting Zena, had said: 'Don't say anything to anybody. I don't want to be noticed.' She thought his shyness might have been due to his lack of height, and she recalled his 'gentle mouth, his hair which was always carefully brushed up into a quiff, and *such eyes*'.

One of Newport's local heroes was the second Viscount Tredegar, who had fought as a captain with the Lancers at the Crimean battle of Balaclava only fifteen years before Davies was born. The boy must often have recited Tennyson's 'Charge of the Light Brigade' and listened fascinated to stories of the viscount's swashbuckling ancestor, Henry Morgan. Morgan was a seventeenth-century buccaneer on the Spanish Main who captured and sacked Panama, later to be knighted and made lieutenant-governor of Jamaica. Consciously or not, Davies's wanderlust may have been imbibed from tales such as Morgan's. He read, he listened and he dreamed of an adventurous future. Even then he had a well-developed sense of his own talents: 'I questioned Nature's wisdom, asking why she did not make two boys of average intelligence, instead of making him so weak of intellect and me so great?' The reference is to his handicapped brother Francis. So at fourteen began Davies's lifelong love of travel and literature and the end of his boyhood.

His first paid job was with an ironmonger, J.P. Sandford in Commercial Street. But this lasted only until his grandfather died in 1886, when the boy was fifteen. His serious-minded Baptist grandmother then had him apprenticed to a Bristol picture-frame carver and gilder, Jeremiah Williams, recommending this as a thoroughly respectable profession. It would seem that from his grandparents he inherited a strong personality, a stubborn streak and a belief in himself. And perhaps from his father he derived artistic talent and from his mother a resilience and a determination to overcome disadvantages. Mary Ann was barely literate, yet she recognized a gift in her son. He invariably returned to see her between his travels and during hard times.

Surprisingly, William Henry stuck to his five-year apprenticeship, but picture-framing did not appeal to him as a profession. He saw himself rather as a globe-trotter, a poet and perhaps an actor. At about this time he read a paper, *In Defence of the Stage*, to a local self-improvement class which he had joined. As a young adult he preferred to spend his time reading and writing poems and cast himself, like many a teenager before and since, in a romantic role. 'I was determined to startle the world somehow or other. For instance, one night when I was looking at the moon, I was struck with the sudden idea that it was the sun changed to a silver hue by the darkness of the night and atmospheric conditions . . . I made a note of this, intending to write a poem on the subject.'

He followed this up by taking a train twenty miles to view an unidentified ruin (almost certainly Tintern Abbey) by moonlight. 'This is worth consideration when it is known that I had worked hard all that day and had to rise early next morning and walk two miles to my work, having to be there at seven o'clock.'[12] He does not record whether the moonlight excursion led to a poem. Most of his poetic output dated from his twenties and thirties; little survives from his teenage years.

The theatre was his dominant interest during his time as an apprentice. Drama was still disapproved of then by many Welsh people, not only chapel-goers. As he said himself, 'I was running a bit wild', and he might have gone to the dogs altogether but for his grandmother's death.

Lydia died in 1891, soon after he had finished his apprenticeship, and her life's savings were put into a trust for the benefit of William and his brother and sister. Each of them was to be paid an equal amount weekly from the trust, administered by a church elder. An advance on this gave Davies the chance to leave Newport for wider horizons, after a brief stay with his mother Mary Ann Hills and her second family, where he clearly felt somewhat *de trop*. He spent six months doing odd jobs in a poor area of Bristol and six months in London apparently living on his allowance.

His Bristol experiences, as an apprentice and a casual labourer, enliven the first chapter of *The True Traveller*. 'I don't know what it is that has always attracted me to ill-dressed people and squalid places. The man that interests me is not the one dressed in the height of fashion, but the bearded man who is wearing three common dirty sacks – one wrapped and tied around each foot, and the other used as a shawl around his neck.'[13] And so it remained for most of his life; wherever he lived or travelled he was irresistibly drawn to the company of tramps, beggars, prostitutes, thieves and wanderers.

Victorian Bristol was a busy port, still home to some families grown rich through earlier slave trading but a far smaller city than it is today. In *The True Traveller* he describes a slum area of Bristol in the 1880s, known as The Pity, where he entered 'a low dirty-looking tavern'. Here the inexperienced lad was caught out by three women playing an old trick, one claiming he was her long-lost son, the others persuading him he so resembled the son of Mary Price that he felt obliged to give her five shillings before he could escape. In Bristol, too, he visited a common lodging-house – the first of many during the next twenty years – and found that he was the only man wearing a collar and tie. Here he was accosted by ragged men claiming to know him. A good deal more crafty by now, he would persuade them to leave him alone by holding out his hat for a whip-round. Davies as a young man was already streetwise long before he set out for North America and able to hold his own in a variety of social situations.

His six months at a loose end in London furthered his knowledge of the life of the poor even more sharply. As he described later in *Beggars*, he started casually by spending two shillings and sixpence a night on bed and breakfast (this would later seem a fortune); then he was robbed, had to make do with meals of tea and bread and butter only and finally forked out a halfpenny on notepaper and another halfpenny on a stamp to write home for more money.[14] After six months he decided that London was not for him and that certainly its alehouses were less desirable for a heavy drinker than the provinces. So he went briefly back to Newport. But he was unsettled, restless and frustrated.

In the end travel beckoned more strongly than commerce or a

steady job, and in 1893, aged twenty-two, he set out for Liverpool to try his luck by working a passage to the USA on a cattle boat. To cross the Atlantic in the 1880s was a serious adventure for a young man. There he was, not long out of his teens, a social rebel with a taste for the illegal (and an even stronger taste for alcohol), well read but ill-disciplined, sporty and artistic, extremely worldlywise, not content to be an ironworker or a picture-framer: a would-be poet looking for a radical way of life. He had been influenced by westerns. He hoped that America might provide what he was looking for.

- 2 -

Down and Out in the USA

Whoever walks the railroad in America will see a curious assortment of
tin cans, in which men have made coffee. He will then know he is in a
beggars' camp . . . If they were true travellers and professional beggars,
the cans will be turned upside down...But if the cans are thrown about
in every direction . . . it can be said with certainty that the camp was
lately occupied by men who are only beggars occasionally, and not
gentlemen.

– Later Days

WHEN W.H. Davies landed at Baltimore in 1893 the USA was going
through one of those periods of depression which alternated with
prosperity after the Civil War – the boom-and-bust cycles. The end of
the war in 1865 was followed by the abolition of slavery in the South,
the assassination of Lincoln and a huge influx of homeless people –
ex-slaves and others – migrating from the South to the northern
industrial areas seeking jobs. Idaho, Montana, South Dakota and
Wyoming had lately joined the Union as the Midwest was settled. The
last major conflict between the US Army and Native Americans had
been the Battle of Wounded Knee in South Dakota, as late as 1891.
The legendary Sitting Bull and 153 other Sioux had been killed. This
was the same Sitting Bull who had been invited to a ceremony to mark
the completion of the Northern Pacific Railway and famously made a
speech in Sioux which included the words 'I hate all white people. You
are thieves and liars.'

It is inconceivable that Davies did not know about Sitting Bull or
his contemporary Crazy Horse, icons of American history, but he
does not mention them. Indeed American history in general seems to
have passed him by. The era of the last freedom-fighting Native Americans was a powerful strain in national mythology, yet the only
mention of these warriors in Davies's published work is a brief reference to Indian camp fires towards the end of *A Poet's Calendar*.[1] He
records his reading of cowboy and western stories as a boy but showed
no apparent curiosity about the cowboys-and-Indians culture of the
Midwest, the Big Country, when he was in the USA. Not all is grist to

a writer's mill, but Davies's work is so repetitive as to suggest a poverty of source material. In fact the reverse was the case.

North America was still a pioneer land, effectively in an era of post-colonial expansion. The seaport of Baltimore in Maryland, one of the earliest European settlements (dating from 1729) and Unionist since 1788, was the major port of entry into the country, with an economy based on shipping, steel and food processing and a population of about 100,000.[2] In spite of its outward prosperity Baltimore had its quota of homeless and unemployed people: refugees from the South, Civil War veterans, European immigrants unable to find work – and all too often unable to speak English.

A seagoing cattleman's life was far from easy. Davies refers to himself as a cattle-stiff, a man who does heavy, dirty and ill-paid work for which he might be paid ten shillings on an Atlantic crossing. However as night-watchman on a cattle ship Davies could earn as much as two pounds. On one such crossing after dark he was startled by a furious cry from the bridge of 'Cover that light, you damn stiff!' The first mate had been annoyed by the lantern Davies was carrying to inspect the cattle. Davies, insulted, retorted that the safety of the ship was no concern of his; he calmed down only when the mate threatened to have him put in irons. He suspected that but for his cattleman's axe he would indeed have been put in chains.

At other times he was actually quite proud to be called a stiff, even a barrel-stiff. 'I have been called a shovel-stiff [a road-worker], a cattle-stiff, and a barrel-house-stiff [a beggar outside pubs], but . . . never a mission-stiff [a beggar outside soup missions].' It seems there was a hierarchy even in terms of occupational abuse.

Davies heard tales of horror in the cattle world. One involved a young stowaway on a ship from England who jumped overboard after being caught, hoping to swim ashore at Baltimore. He was carried out to sea, rescued after two days in the water and sent to gaol. Another cattleman had insulted a Kentucky woman whose husband led a gang planning to lynch him. He was saved from hanging by a sympathetic witness who spoke up even as they were tightening the rope around the man's neck.

Between occasional crossings on cattle ships Davies found himself one of an army of vagrants, tramps and men sleeping rough. Whether he knew what to expect when he arrived in the USA is doubtful. He would have heard some travellers' tales from sailors and fellow passengers, but his knowledge of the homeless American's way of life was probably confined to reading a few westerns and the stories of the best-selling Californian author Jack London. In *The Road* and *The Tramp* London gave accounts of the perils of begging in the 1880s. He wrote of a typical tramp: 'When out of work and still discouraged he has been forced to "hit the road" between large cities in his quest for a job.'[3] Other writers at once took issue with London. The man he was describing, they argued, was not a tramp but a hobo. Davies falls somewhere between the two categories, at times picking up odd jobs, at other times unemployed from choice.

Much has been written by sociologists about the American tramp. He first appeared in literature in the 1870s, his numbers swelled by railroad strikers and ex-slaves. Around the turn of the century it was reckoned there might have been 350,000 professional wanderers on the roads in the USA; one of them was Davies. Of this number it was calculated that more than three-fifths were American-born, one-fifth Irish, the rest made up of English, Germans and Italians.

Broadly speaking, American society recognized three categories of the mobile and mainly unemployed: hoboes, or travelling casual workers; tramps, travelling non-workers; and bums, non-travelling non-workers. Within these groups came unequal sub-divisions: organ-grinders, knife-sharpeners, limbless men (many of them war-disabled), women tramps, rattlers (who rode on freight trains) and ramblers (who preferred passenger trains), the very old and prostitutes.

The Kansas Vagrancy Act around the turn of the century specified: 'All beggars and vagabonds who roam about from place to place, sleeping in barns, sheds, outhouses or in the open air, not giving a good account of themselves . . . shall be deemed vagrants and liable to the penalties of the act.'

Davies initially qualified as a hobo, the name deriving probably from hoe-boy or itinerant farm worker. His original intention was to work, and there is no evidence that he considered begging as a way of life until he fell in with some congenial job-seekers in Baltimore, his port of entry to the USA. He liked Baltimore and its people, writing later that he would have been content to spend his winters idling there and his summers 'travelling through the green country'. It appealed to him as an innovative and civilized place. It was also a terminus of the first American railroad. Samuel Morse set up the first electric telegraph between Baltimore and Washington; and the Johns Hopkins was one of the first universities.

In the 1890s cattle boats crossed the Atlantic several times a week from Baltimore to Liverpool, Glasgow or Cork. They carried in a year anything up to a hundred million pounds of beef, heading for European markets, and most returning more or less empty. The beef was mainly shipped on the hoof because of limited cold-storage facilities for meat. In some cases good-quality British cattle were shipped in the opposite direction, from Britain, to replenish American breeding stock. Fit young men from Europe worked their passage out by doing menial tasks on board; then they accumulated cash by picking up temporary farm work, building railroads or undertaking construction jobs in the fast-developing Midwest, finally working their way back to Europe looking after the travelling livestock. This was at first what Davies planned to do; to join the army of itinerant cattlemen.

A hundred years later Baltimore has forgotten Davies, although his books are lodged in a few university libraries there, and a Baltimore academic told the author his son treasured an early edition of Davies's first verse collection, *The Soul's Destroyer* (reissued in 1922). The son had also been given a copy of *The Autobiography of a Super-Tramp* because of a teen interest in a rock group called Supertramp, best known for their song 'Breakfast in America'. Whether the band's name derived from the book or from more general hearsay is uncertain.

Baltimore bred its own literary heroes: H.L. Mencken, social philosopher, much-admired writer and editor for twenty years of the *Baltimore Sun,* who was born there; and Edgar Allan Poe, exponent *par excellence* of tales of mystery, who was buried there. A transient non-American who later wrote briefly about Baltimore in the 1890s would be unlikely to generate much interest.

Another of the city's claims to fame was its defence of Fort McHenry against the British in 1814, which inspired Francis Scott Key's famous anthem 'The Star-Spangled Banner'. Davies never mentions these Baltimore heroes, although he must have heard them discussed in the bars and hostels where he loitered and made friends. As a writer his eye was fixed firmly on the road.

Baltimore was the lynchpin of a huge movement of cattle and the eastern terminus of the Baltimore to Ohio Railroad, the first railway in all of America. It was opened in 1830. The station, where Davies spent many hours waiting for a free ride or helping to unload the cattle cars, is now a railroad museum. Among its exhibits are replicas of steam trains from his era. By his time pioneers had opened up the western plains way beyond Ohio, then spearheaded into the Great Plains, towards the Rockies and the Sierra Nevada. At first these areas where the buffalo once roamed were primarily the terrain of surviving Plains Indian tribes. Then came pioneer miners and ranchers. Gradually new agricultural techniques tamed the dry lands and farming settlers started to put down roots, pioneers of the prairie states.

In 1862 Congress passed the Pacific Railroad Act, opening the way for a 'ribbon of steel' from the Atlantic to the Pacific, providing contact between the settlers and their kinsfolk back along the east coast. After the Civil War railroads mushroomed, and when Davies arrived in 1893 the lines of the Union Pacific (from the west) and Central Pacific (from the east) had lately met at Promontory Point, Utah, forming a 1,750-mile link across the USA. The builders held a ceremony with a gold spike to fix the last rail in place. The Northern Pacific ran from Minnesota to North Dakota; the Santa Fe Railroad extended from Chicago to the Gulf of Mexico; the Southern Pacific stretched from Texas to Arizona; and a cluster of lesser lines crisscrossed the USA, many centring on Chicago. Mighty railroads networked the nation and symbolized the character of the growing post-war America. This was a period of prosperity, but it did not last. Bitter winters and long droughts hit the cattle barons hard, forcing many of them to give up farming.

Ranchers from Texas, however, did prosper, feeding their cattle cheaply on the grasslands further north, then transporting the prime animals to the booming towns and ports of the eastern states. The poorly paid drovers or cattle-herders might be Civil War veterans, ex-slaves from the South or – like Davies – immigrants looking for adventure. They had to swim the animals across rivers, protect them from cattle rustlers and feed themselves on the way. But the growth of the railways gradually cut down this source of income for many of the homeless, who inevitably took to the road.

As well as passengers, the new steam trains started to carry grain and livestock. Few settlements on the lines were without a station, a telegraph and mail office or a basic shop. Saloons, brothels and casinos provided cheap entertainment for the single travelling male. Companies such as Wells, Fargo ran stagecoaches from every station. And these became the focal points for unemployed men or casual labourers seeking work – or, like Davies, begging. They also made it easier for bank and train robbers to make a quick get-away. The railroads were both an escape route and a death trap for adventurers.

Begging in America was an almost legitimate lifestyle, far less despised than in England. The word 'tramp' became part of the language around 1870, and within thirty years there was public recognition of the tramp population, as well as a vague suspicion. People living in isolated country areas saw the tramp as 'a shiftless idle hooligan who avoided work at all costs', but most tramps were in fact hoboes, picking up casual work where they could. They slept in all kinds of places: bunkhouses near rail stations or lumber camps, woodland clearings, missions, police stations or, a shade more luxuriously, in city lodging-houses. These were usually set up by philanthropists, with strict rules for the inmates. Nobody would be admitted who was the worse for drink; drinking, smoking and swearing were forbidden; a stay was limited to three days. Most unpopular for the hobo was the rule that insisted on each inmate sawing a pile of wood in part payment for his food. A sleeping cubicle would typically cost twenty-five cents a night, a place on the communal floor ten cents.[4]

Techniques of begging were as varied as the beggars. 'American beggars knock boldly at doors like kings' messengers,' wrote Davies in *The Adventures of Johnny Walker, Tramp*. An imposing mansion with marble pillars would be bypassed by an English beggar, but his opposite number in the USA would regard it as a challenge. The successful American beggar would boast of having conned a president, an actor or a prize fighter. Davies puzzled over the average American's generosity. Some, however, would ask the beggar to chop some wood in return for food; amazing, he noted, how quickly the beggar would break the axe-handle.

Davies at first had some idea of searching for regular work inland, but this was soon abandoned in favour of life on the road: 'seeking to improve my mind and body as a tramp,' he claimed. At no time was there any suggestion that he was sightseeing or collecting material to write about. And, surprisingly, there is no evidence that he ever kept a diary. His ambition was always to be a writer, but he made no practical preparation for such a life. He showed no inclination to educate himself further, although the state of Maryland was early in providing free schools and as well as reading-rooms and libraries. As it did for George Borrow a generation earlier in England, it was 'the wind on the heath, brother' that irresistibly attracted Davies. With a little rhetoric a hobo's life could even be defended as respectable.

He learned the way of the road from a chance Baltimore acquaintance, Brum from Birmingham, who persuaded Davies to bum with him to Chicago. Brum taught Davies many tricks of the trade which he had picked up after arriving in the USA. One was to beg in the neighbourhood of a Catholic church; another was to aim for the area of a town with a mill, a factory or a brewery rather than comfortable homes. In summer the hoboes made for seaside resorts, where holidaymakers might or might not be generous. Things did not always go smoothly. Trespassing on the railroad, illegally boarding a train or loitering at a station were all imprisonable offences.

Prison, however, was a desirable objective when bitter weather overtook the freeriders. In Michigan Davies and Brum negotiated with the town marshal for a thirty-day sentence plus some tobacco and a dollar or two. Publicly it was arranged they would be arrested for being drunk and disorderly, so that they could spend thirty days inside in relative comfort.[5]

Davies found the techniques easy and the life attractive. The beggar's first task on reaching the outskirts of a town was to look for some woodland, water and 'an assortment of tin cans in which men have made coffee'. This signalled a regular tramps' camp, often with a fire kept always burning under a stewpot. Tins turned upside down to prevent them rusting indicated full-time tramps, who often carved their names on the trees – almost a mark of ownership. Tins thrown about all over the place suggested what Davies called 'gay cats' or part-time or rogue tramps. In such a place he met Detroit Fatty,

Saginaw Slim and Harlem Baldy. (The nicknames of tramps generally gave a clue both to their home place and their physical appearance. Davies must have intrigued them with his Welsh accent and his fastidious dress, although it is not known what they called him.) Later acquaintances were Frisco Fatty, Cincinatti Slim and Boston Shorty. He learned from these three how to listen for the midday factory hooter, to wait for workers to start their meal and then set out to beg hot food from them while they ate.

On one occasion Detroit Fatty startled his mates by showing acute remorse over a stolen bar of soap, which in his eyes branded him a common thief. His mates put it down to a fit of temporary insanity. Davies puzzled over how such a successful professional beggar could stoop so low when he could have begged half a ton of soap in a day.

Some of his tales of begging in the USA verge on the apocryphal. One concerned an adventure of Boston Shorty, who marched boldly to the top floor of a tenement building and asked for breakfast as if he were the landlord or a rent collector. He was given buckwheat cakes and coffee. An hour or two later he called impudently at the second floor of the same house, where the door was opened by the same woman. Instead of berating him for his cheek she asked her friend to give him dinner. In the evening he repeated the trick downstairs, apparently with complete success.

At a house on Long Island Sound, where the wanderers gathered in summer, Davies was advised by this same Shorty not to address the housewife as 'Lady', a common mode of address used by tramps. This was because the woman considered men who did so to be professional beggars. Those who called her 'Madam' were perceived as gentlemen.

Davies's article 'The Camp', a section in his 1925 book *Later Days*, was written by a waterfall on Long Island Sound, where he spent many summer nights in the open: perhaps the happiest period of his hobo days. As early as this the poet's eye was in evidence: the camp was sited by a 'freshwater spring, at its very source, where it is seen as a large eye with tears running down the face of a dark rock'. Summertime, he reflected, meant the tramps had only to beg for food; in winter they would have 'to work a little harder and longer' for the price of a night's bed.

Davies was a less shrewd amateur psychologist than Boston Shorty and his friend Brum. At a smalltown Texas boarding-house by a sawmill he was given a hot meal and, to his dismay, interrogated by the sawmill manager. The upshot of this was not that he was arrested, as he feared, but offered a well-paid job at the mill. He wriggled out of this predicament by saying he was a tailor on his way to a job in Houston.

The hazards of the travelling life were not so much a cause of alarm as a rich source of anecdotal material for later use. Davies was inordinately proud of his prowess as a boxer, dating back to his schooldays. 'I carried a most deadly punch everywhere I went,' he boasted. He also acquired quite legally and carried a six-chamber revolver on his way to New Orleans, and this nearly led to his death. He tells this story in *Later Days*:

> I was suddenly attacked by several men. One of them struck me such a heavy blow on the side of the head that I heard birds singing in my ears immediately . . . When I recovered my senses my left eye was closed fast and the other had a little light, about the size of a canary seed. I was so weak that the blood I lost would probably have made enough black-pudding to feed a small family. But what annoyed me most was the loss of my six deadly punches.

He carried the scars of the adventure for life, with a broken bridge to his nose and a permanent swelling under his left eye, and remained always childishly proud of his skill with his fists: 'A prizefighter without a punch is no more than cabbage without boiled beef, or a dish of beans without pork.'

In *The Adventures of Johnny Walker, Tramp*, Davies mentions that after the end of the World's Fair in Chicago there were thousands of men out of work resorting, as he did, to charity soup kitchens. At one such he was surprised to see the bowls of soup given out by a number of well-dressed women. His companion told him that it was a sporting house, in other words a brothel: 'You can always rely on girls of that kind to do something good for the poor, and they do not make the soup cold with hymns and prayers.' This was a theme Davies often returned to throughout his life, the kindness and generosity of prostitutes, who fascinated him.

His opinion of Tennessee was not high. At one prosperous but isolated house three peaceful beggars, including Davies, were threatened by a farmer with a shotgun. They resorted to stealing bread and bacon and leaving a dollar bill in payment – 'four times the worth of what we had taken'. But there was loss of face in having actually to pay for food.

A novel written years later, *Dancing Mad*, reflects something of his hand-to-mouth existence in following the Mississippi down river.[6] The hero, an artist called Norman, buys a boat and drifts downstream, camping at night. There are echoes of Mark Twain in this section of the book. Norman catches malaria in the swamps and nearly dies, as Davies did, jumps a train to Memphis and gets involved in several unsavoury fights. Critics have pointed to a number of instances of racism in Davies's writing. In this story he recommends, apparently seriously, the death penalty for blacks ('niggers') who steal chickens, and he gives a very full one-sided account of whites fighting blacks in the Southern states. This of course was fifty years before the growth of the Civil Rights movement. Davies makes no attempt to hide his racial prejudice, something he carried with him all his life. The word 'nigger' crops up in several of his books, and he shows prejudice also towards the Chinese.

The True Traveller describes the preferred use of razors as weapons in the deep South, used with as much skill as Englishmen practising boxing or fencing. This leads to a grisly report on the mutilation of black faces in razor fights and the surprising information (especially coming from Davies, who regarded women nervously and with some awe) that black women he had met carried razors inside their stockings. Long after his American travels he engaged in debate with other tramps about the relative merits of razors, as opposed to the use of fists, knives or revolvers in fights. There are references to Frisco Slim and Denver Red – possibly he invented the names and the exploits – experts at shooting with a pistol through a coat pocket, undetected. From the manner of his telling these travellers' tales one deduces that Davies still had a boyish delight at being involved in fights. He was pugnacious, physically strong and not easily outfaced.

In spite of a tramp's natural disinclination to work, he admits that sometimes he felt 'inclined to break the monotony by doing a little light labour', which was how he found himself signing on at a fruit farm near Galveston, Texas. This was run by a Chinese syndicate. Davies was instructed to pick only the best strawberries, those with a little stem. The berries proved hard to find, so the Welshman and Brum stayed only a short while. (This anecdote, in which he resorts to a mocking imitation of Chinese speech, has also been viewed as an instance of Davies's racism.)

And so his adventures went on to and fro across the USA, through Texas, Tennessee, Arkansas and Mississippi, up north to Illinois and New England, for nearly six years. Apart from occasional trips back to Wales he spent most of these years on the road in America. Sleeping rough under the night sky put him at risk from snakes, wild boar, birds of prey and polluted water. He was attacked by a swarm of beetles in a wood and encountered a seven-foot snake hanging from a tree. Fortunately for him it was dead. That he enjoyed this precarious way of life is implicit in nearly all his autobiographical writings. He was fit, unafraid of chance encounters, and when it came to begging his Welsh accent and plausibility worked well for him. Unlike some of the indigenous hoboes he made a point of always being clean, well shaven and reasonably dressed. He loved the open air, observing wild life, building camp fires at night, but above all he was intrigued and entertained by the company of his fellow travellers. What they made of him we have no means of knowing, but it seems possible they found him an amusing oddball and even perhaps a kind of protégé, as British literary celebrities were to regard him twenty years later.

Now and then he found himself in trouble with police, railwaymen and decent American citizens. More than once he was very ill in hospital. What motivated him to persist in this precarious way of life? It seems that he revelled in the freedom and the outdoor life, and it was easier to keep bumming along than to make the effort to settle down. The gentlemen of the road were his friends, and it was in his nature to run risks.

Nights were the hardest. In cities, if there was no cheap hostel, space might be available on let-down beds, a dozen to a room, in police stations. In fine weather a dry open space under trees, near the railroad and within reach of houses or a small store, would do very well for bed and breakfast even if there was no regular camp. A photograph from

1895 shows a crowd of youngish men (none much over forty) mostly in suits and bowler-hatted (no ties) sitting round a stewpot near a camp fire.[7] They have a contented, almost prosperous air, although they are clearly camera-shy. Dogs, pipes and walrus moustaches are common accoutrements. Photographs taken at a wayfarers' lodge in Boston in 1897 illustrate communal washing in tubs and lining up for breakfast bowls. A tramp posing for a studio portrait in 1893 ('Roving Bill') carries the tools of his trade (mending umbrellas), wears a derby hat and smokes what looks like a clay pipe.

The American tramp was elevated to cult status by Charlie Chaplin, with the coming of the silent movies. *The Tramp,* in 1915, and *The Gold Rush,* in 1925, established the melancholy character of the Little Tramp, with his big boots, baggy trousers and too small battered hat, an icon of the early cinema. The image owed a lot to clowns, but Chaplin said that it had its roots in an actual tramp he met in San Francisco.[8] The American tramp was seen as a sad comic rather than an outcast, a fantasist and a romantic, waiting for something to turn up. Outwardly he seemed a more gentlemanly traveller than his British contemporary. Davies in this role had no reason to feel socially inferior, if indeed he ever did.

After a brief spell in London he was back on the road again in America from 1895 to 1897, his paths crossing those of old begging acquaintance such as Australian Red and Frisco Fatty. Inevitably they attracted trouble. In Tennessee three of them took to the back roads, away from settled towns, and ran out of food – although they had money. They made for a planter's house and threatened him with a revolver while they helped themselves to food. They hid the farmer's gun and gave him money to cover the cost of what they had stolen. This seems at first out of character for Davies until one remembers his history as a wayward adolescent.

But to Davies this was a minor adventure compared with the wild hog incident in Arkansas. Four beggars set up camp and lit a fire to cook bacon, tomatoes and corncobs, but the camp was invaded by ferocious hogs who lived up to their name and helped themselves to the beggars' supper. Elsewhere Davies saw a frightened hog run over by a train. He had a poor opinion of the people of Arkansas ('the most unenlightened people of America . . . Books and newspapers they know little of'). The skins of hunted hogs were exchanged for clothes, ammunition, coffee and tobacco. Arkansas houses on stilts, entered by a ladder, were 'more like large pigeon-coops'. Some of them, he wrote with scorn, regarded a store, a railway station and five or six houses as a town, and one well-spoken man patronizingly asked him to say something in his own language. Davies remembered the area mainly as swampland, overrun by snakes and flies.

Some of his strangest and most unconvincing American tales were of his encounters with prostitutes. He usually refers to them as women of fashion or sometimes courtesans; brothels are 'sporting houses'. His relations with women remained ambiguous for most of his life. They both fascinated and frightened him. Always he was more at ease with women who were his social inferiors, happier in groups than with individual women and apparently alarmed by those who made sexual advances to him. In Illinois, railroad-riding, he left a train overnight at a siding and set up camp in a wood.[9] At three in the morning a well-dressed woman appeared, apparently collecting firewood. Davies dressed hurriedly. She sat by his fire till morning, telling him her life story, and invited him to join her at one Carrie Watson's House in Chicago ('a fashionable sporting house'). According to the author, she made no attempt to seduce him and went away quietly when the sun came up.

Another of these passionless encounters happened after he contracted malaria in the Mississippi swamps, tried to reach a hospital and could get no further than a bar where he dosed himself with neat whisky. A kind woman put him to bed, fetched a doctor and medicine and even read to him while he was recovering. As usual Davies claims he did not for some time recognize her as a prostitute. This adventure caused him to reflect sympathetically on how such women manage to survive in old age. For most of his life Davies was intrigued by the profession and wrote often about the 'courtesans' he met on both sides of the Atlantic.

After four years on the road Davies made his way back to Baltimore and signed on for a crossing on the cattle ship *Concordia*, which involved waiting for a few days in the port: time for yet another strange encounter. No bars were officially open on a Sunday, so he was asked by two apparently well-to-do men to point them towards a speak-easy.

He led them to 'a low-grade quarter called the Mash Market', where they drank heavily and illegally. Their next inquiry was for Alice Ann Street, which Davies knew to be Baltimore's red-light quarter. The picture then is confused, involving drugged wine, robbery and Davies being threatened by a woman with a revolver because he said he had no money. ('Open the door, or I'll blow his brains out!') He escaped, and heard later that the well-heeled strangers had been robbed of two hundred dollars. It is hard to decide whether Davies was naively lucky or sharper than he admits.

The *Concordia* sailed for Glasgow, taking twelve to fourteen days. One of the commonest of casual jobs was supervising cattle on their long journeys by land or sea. Hitherto breeders in the West had had to drive their prime cattle overland to the markets of the big cities: New York, Philadelphia, Baltimore. Now the railroads made it possible to transport whole herds rapidly and economically. Dodge City in Kansas was the 'Queen of the Cow Towns'. Chicago had huge slaughtering and meat-packing facilities for beef to be shipped by railway wagon to the ports, and several times a week the cattle on the hoof arrived in Baltimore.

Davies in his *Autobiography* gives an alarming account of a cattleman's job at the port. The cattle, often wild, had to be forced through a narrow passage where nooses were tied on their necks or horns. Then they were driven or dragged on board ship, up a narrow gangway, by prodding them with sharp poles. The terrified cattle were in danger of falling overboard or goring one of the cattlemen, whose next job was to fasten them to posts where they stayed standing throughout the voyage. (If they knelt or lay down there was a risk of the ropes getting entwined or a valuable animal strangled. The most effective if painful way to force a lying cow to stand up was to twist its tail.)

Once he had mastered the tricky business of securing the cows without serious injury to man or beast, Davies was appointed night watchman. This involved dealing single-handedly with cattle that had worked themselves loose, bellowing and slithering about on deck. After a few days at sea – with luck – the animals would calm down.[10] On one such voyage two thousand sheep were also carried, packed together on an upper deck, and a severe storm swept half of them

overboard.Worse still, according to Davies: 'It is every morning necessary to crawl through the pens, far back, in quest of the sick and dead
[sheep], and it is nothing unusual to find half a dozen dead ones.' His
pay for this physically demanding two-week voyage was thirty shillings
and a return ticket to Baltimore, or whichever port he had sailed from,
on an empty cattleboat. His unhappy experiences at sea with sheep
inspired his poem 'Sheep', but there is little other reference in the
poems to the horror of these voyages.

Often Davies would pass the time in his bunk reading and smoking. This must have amazed his fellow cattlemen, regarded by many –
although not by him – as 'the riff-raff of America and the scum of
Europe'. He tells a tale of thieves, card-sharpers, conmen and chronic
liars, yet he enjoyed their company and stored up their anecdotes, perhaps for future use. His writings never suggest any sense of superiority
over them. Whether hard-luck cases or rogues, these men were his
brothers, on the road or on board ship.

On one return voyage there was no work for the cattlemen except
to fetch food from the galley and swab down the decks, with two men
each day allotted to these tasks. A fifteenth man spent the entire crossing lying on his bunk. When they reached Baltimore the man could
hardly walk, through long inactivity (possibly a euphemism for two
weeks' drinking), and his mates had to fork out five cents for a car to
get him to the cattlemen's office where they all had to sign on.

Some gaps in Davies's account need to be filled in. The crossing of
the north Atlantic took at least a fortnight, often in foul weather, and
icebergs were often sighted. This was more than a decade before the
sinking of the *Titanic*; Davies was well aware how much icebergs were
feared by sailors. During severe storms at sea cattlemen might be
killed by timber coming adrift, and they were hard put to survive
between crossings on the pittance they earned. Most of it went on
drink ashore. Food on board was meagre, and the men slept in
cramped bunks below deck. Some were paid as little as ten shillings a
crossing.

In the early 1890s Davies made four cattleboat crossings, but with
spring and better weather coming he opted for a wandering life on
land and kept this up for five years. Soon bored with New York, he
moved on to Connecticut and fell in with some old begging hands

who urged him to join them. His first Christmas in Baltimore had given him a taste for begging: working well-off neighbourhoods with two experienced beggars he had picked up sixty food parcels, some packed with such delicacies as oysters, turkey, beef, mutton, fruit, tarts, cakes and pies. This was during a time of economic depression when unemployment was widespread, but when he reached Chicago Davies quickly found casual labour on the half-built Chicago Ship Canal as an assistant cook and bottle-washer. He slept in the open air through an earthquake without knowing it, drifted down the Mississippi from St Louis in a houseboat, witnessed a murder during a razor fight near New Orleans and contracted swamp fever near Memphis.

These journeys of his covered ten states and some four thousand miles, long before the days of backpackers, hitchhikers or organized campsites. He worked or begged his way through time zones and extremes of climate, working out of his system (or so he imagined) the wanderlust he had perhaps inherited from his seagoing forebears. The railways were the wonder of the age, and Davies exploited them to the full. 'All tramps in America travel on the railroad, whether they walk or take free rides,' he wrote. From his friend Brum he learned that railroad depots offered good resources for scrounging food, since most tramps avoided hanging around them, and good sleeping quarters too.

In the summer Davies and his fellow travellers made for Long Island Sound, in New York State, enjoying the seaside life almost as much as the wealthy New Yorkers who had beach houses there. From there they moved on to New Haven, where they made the mistake of begging in the street, instead of from house to house, and ended up serving a thirty-day sentence in gaol. Even this was not unpleasant; they were set to light labour caning chairs and pampered with a good supply of tobacco. Part of the explanation may be that sheriffs or gaolers were paid so many dollars for each arrest they made, so tramps were popular.

Begging his way south again, Davies joined forces for a time with a bunch of lively and heavy-drinking beggars in Philadelphia. Finally he did a stint of fruit-picking in Illinois, but a sudden overpowering desire to return home came over him, triggered by reading some

Robert Burns poems. So he spent most of his fruit-picking earnings – over a hundred dollars – on a week-long binge in Chicago and set off for Wales via the Baltimore and Ohio Railroad and yet another cattle-boat to Liverpool. Five years on the road in the USA had matured him, made him worldlywise beyond his years and given him a lifelong weakness for drink and tobacco. Add to this his extreme canniness about money, his fascination with whores, yet his nervousness in their company, and his casual attitude to injury or physical hardship: this was Davies at the age of twenty-seven.

Curiously, although he wrote thousands of words in prose about his North American adventures, only two or three of his seven hundred poems refer to them directly. 'Baltimore' (elsewhere he gave it the title 'Sheep') describes in moving and simplistic style his signing on to escort 1,800 sheep 'from Baltimore to Glasgow town' by sea, for fifty shillings in advance. At first the sheep were calm:

> The first night we were out at sea
> Those sheep were quiet in their mind;
> The second night they cried with fear –
> They smelt no pastures in the wind.
> They sniffed, poor things, for their green fields,
> They cried so loud I could not sleep:
> For fifty thousand shillings down
> I would not sail again with sheep.

The same topic reappears in 'A Child's Pet', written much later. On one such voyage a single sheep displayed no fear of the sea or the sailors. The author deduced that it had once been a pet lamb:

> So every time we passed it by,
> Sailing to England's slaughter-house,
> Eight ragged sheep-men – tramps and thieves –
> Would stroke that sheep's black nose.

Analysis of Davies's poems reveals that sheep are mentioned more than any other animal, but more often as sentimental objects in a landscape rather then living breathing creatures. All his life Davies was

49

an animal-lover with a tendency to credit animals with human emotions, and in later years he was never without a pet dog or cat. However, sheep and cows are observed, in prose and poetry, only as far as he had immediate experience of them, and clearly his experience did not extend to Welsh farming or even cattle-ranching in the USA. If he had worked on one of the great Midwest ranches, or helped to drive vast herds of cattle hundreds of miles across the plains to such railroad depots as Kansas City, Dodge City or Montana, one would expect some realistic reflection of farming life or livestock handling. An ever-present danger on the road was the possibility of a herd stampeding, scared by freak weather conditions, a frisky horse, or difficult river crossings. Death of men and animals was a daily occurrence, although seldom mentioned by Davies.

The cattle trail ended at the railhead. Cattle hands prodded steers up a ramp into cattle cars for shipment to market. It was a brutal industry, and it calls for imagination to envisage Davies, the diminutive Welsh city lad, in the type of scenes made popular in cowboy films. Yet there he was, a tough little man among the cattle giants, thirty years before the cinema made them familiar. This was when the West was still opening up and pioneers were struggling to survive in a harsh frontier country.

His own struggle to survive in the 1890s is merely hinted at in the *Autobiography*, *The True Traveller* and *The Adventures of Johnny Walker, Tramp*. Nowhere does he realistically convey the constant risks of this hazardous way of life. In *Later Days* he paints some thumbnail sketches of life on the American road, the men he fell in with and their relations with settled American citizens. But these are little more than loosely linked anecdotes.

In an apparently unpublished article written in about 1914 he wrote: 'I went off to America in my twenty-first year and wandered as a tramp there for six years. In all that time I did not read more than six books. Sometimes I picked up a newspaper thrown out of a railway carriage, which I read when I camped in the woods . . . In spite of this, my dream of a literary life never left me for a whole day. But if I had not gone all that time without reading books of good poetry, who knows what I could have been [at] the present day? Perhaps a Professor of Poetry!'[11]

If there was rich material waiting to be recorded from this period of his life, it found its way mainly into the *Autobiography* and in such a low-key manner that it is hard to realize how often Davies confronted death. His other prose works either cover the same ground or add no more than footnotes to it. He was an acutely observant lyric poet and a good objective reporter but not a truly creative prose writer.

He arrived back in Newport in November 1896 with three shillings left from his earnings. The town and the docks were bigger, modernized and not easy to recognize. His mother had moved and both his grandparents had died, but a former neighbour directed him to his mother's place. She greeted him warmly with '"I thought it was your knock", just as though I had only been out for an evening's stroll'. Although he had seen relatively little of his mother since her second marriage, Davies retained a real affection for her. However, his stay in Newport lasted only a few weeks. A comfortable bed and good cooking did not appeal after life in the open air. Much of his accumulated legacy went on drink. His old school friends seemed to be leading dull and unenterprising lives. A trip on a local cargo boat to Bordeaux did nothing to cure his wanderlust; nor did a brief spell in London, where he considered opening a bookshop with what remained of his grandmother's legacy.

He saw several empty shops that might have suited his purpose, but there remained a problem. 'I had not the least notion of how or where to obtain books . . . if I could have bought a bookshop ready fitted and filled, no doubt I would have closed with the offer at once, and settled quietly down.' The reader can only speculate on how different his writings would have been. Instead he spent his days walking the city and his evenings at the theatre. This was the end of the 1890s, a golden age in the music halls, the era of Wilde, Pinero, Gilbert and Sullivan. George Bernard Shaw was midway into his long career as a dramatist; *Widowers' Houses* had appeared in 1892. There was plenty to satisfy Davies's appetite for the theatre, and seats in the gods, or standing room, could be had a for a few pence. He was content for a while to be a Londoner.

Then he chanced upon a copy of a London newspaper, the *Evening Standard,* which carried a report of the Klondyke Gold Rush.[12] The idea of prospecting for gold in the far north of Canada was irresistible, not because he wanted to be hugely rich ('all I desired was a small house of my own, and leisure for study') but because in his fantasy he saw himself with a collection of gold nuggets worth £2,000, wealth enough to become a serious student of literature.

Impulsively in early 1899, with little money and few belongings, he sailed for St John's, New Brunswick, from where he planned to travel on his own across Canada: the second phase of his life as a hobo.

Down and Very Much Out in Canada

I now found that my right foot was severed from the ankle . . . When I
was placed in a waiting room to bide the arrival of a doctor, I could see
no other way of keeping a calm face than by taking out my pipe and
smoking, an action which I am told caused much sensation in the local
press.

– The Autobiography of a Super-Tramp

CANADA in the late years of the nineteenth century was still an emer-
gent country, with few major towns more than fifty years old. In the
year that Davies was born Edmonton was little more than a defended
trading post. Canada's history was changed dramatically by the coming of railroads, the spread of farming and the finding of gold along
the foothills of the Rockies. The first major gold strike was in the
Fraser River valley in the 1850s – the Caribou Gold Rush. Goldfield
after goldfield was worked out, but the prospectors moved on north
and new settlements sprang up from Vancouver to the Yukon.

This Gold Rush was the overwhelming attraction of Canada for
emigrants in the 1890s. From California to Alaska gold fever had been
contagious for nearly fifty years. Mining towns sprang up wherever a
lode or a few nuggets were spotted, although for many of them boom
was quickly followed by bust. Prospectors and miners rushed to each
new camp where rumours of ore circulated, always optimistic, for ever
expecting to make a fortune.

A few did; most slaved at site after site for a few handfuls of dust.
Whether Davies would have done well as a prospector is open to
doubt. Opportunism alone was not enough. The few who struck lucky
needed considerable geological and technical know-how. Life in the
mining camps was harsh and rough in the extreme, but plenty of
female company, entertainment and liquor were available in the
shanty towns, and enterprising fit men who could resist throwing
away their finds on drink could make enough to settle down and set up
home. And this was Davies's dream: to have money to own a home
and books.

In 1896 there was an appeal for 'stalwart peasants in sheepskin coats, born on the soil' to come as settlers to the prairie lands. So they flooded in from the Ukraine, Germany, Holland and Poland to swell the mainly French and English communities and the indigenous peoples, today called the First Nations. This was the young enterprising country Davies now looked towards.

Also in the 1890s came news of a new strike in the far north-west of Canada, in the valley of the Klondike river in the Yukon; a strike productive enough to attract 30,000 people in the next fifteen years. It was this dream of Eldorado that the 28-year-old Davies read about in that London evening paper under the headline 'A Land of Gold'.[1] All thoughts of settling down and running a bookshop went out of the window. Next day he set out by train for Liverpool with £44 in a money-belt, the remains of his grandmother's legacy, reckoning that this plus some train-hitching would get him to the Yukon. It was all he had. Call it folly, crazy optimism or naivety; for a time gold fever gripped him.

He already knew a little of Canada from crossing the Great Lakes to and fro from the Chicago side, as many ex-sailors or cattlemen did in summer. Davies wrote: 'On their deep-sea boats they get hard biscuits, salt meat, dried peas and cheap molasses; but on the lakes they get soft bread, fresh meat, green vegetables and luxurious fruit. It is no lie that common sailors and firemen on the American lakes get strawberries and cream.' He found that ex-merchant navy seamen or former navy sailors could not resist the lure of good food and easy jobs as crewmen on the Great Lakes in summer, earning enough to see them through the winter.[2]

Years later he told in *The Adventures of Johnny Walker, Tramp* how difficult he found it to resist this temptation: freshwater sailors did not need to buy oilskins, special gear or topboots; their life was cushy in comparison with life at sea, and he had had some experience of this too. He haunted the lakeside cities – Chicago, Cleveland, Buffalo, Toronto – where he could be sure of a few dollars from old friends in return for help he had given them in Baltimore or elsewhere.

So in the mid-1890s he had made for Toronto to seek work on a Lakes steamer but was seduced, as so often, by the ease of begging in the city. He relaxed on a grassy common, where both breakfast and dinner were easy to come by and the people unusually kind. He even played ball and skipping games with children on the common. This good life came to an end rather abruptly when he was unexpectedly refused food at one dwelling. The man of the house attacked him for playing with children instead of looking for honest work. Despite this his wife gave Davies a meal, but he left the city hurriedly in case the husband reported him to the police – an example of his habit of taking the line of least resistance, since he had arrived in Toronto genuinely intending to get work on a steamer.

He vividly describes the violent storms which could blow up even on these usually calm inland lakes: 'One winter I went down to the waterside to see a ship in its last extremity. When I got there I saw thousands of helpless people watching a vessel sinking before their eyes, no one being able to go to their assistance in small boats.'[3]

When, in the early spring of 1899, he reached St John, New Brunswick, he was unable to get any further because the St Lawrence River, the waterway to Montreal, was still icebound. This was before icebreakers were used to keep the river navigable in winter. Since he needed all his money for future contingencies, he had no choice but to spend three or four days in St John, before trying to 'beat his way' to Montreal overland: a distance of some four hundred miles.

Davies's patronizing references to Jewish refugees and Russian peasants among his fellow steerage passengers on board the emigrant ship have given rise to some criticism; he found these eastern Europeans crude and not too concerned about personal hygiene ('a low class . . . without the least thought of washing . . . hiding food in their bed clothes').[4] These are by no means the only instances of racism which have been held against him (see pp. 42–3). Bearing in mind his conventional upbringing and the social hierarchy that existed even among beggars, his occasional intolerance is none too surprising. One hundred years ago political correctness was not in vogue.

Five Englishmen and a Frenchman decided to appropriate a table on board ship and started a fight to throw out 'these usurpers . . . haters of soap and water'. Landing at St John, he was much offended to be addressed by a customs officer in an unfamiliar language. Davies supposed this to be because of his dark features and complexion, but perhaps unwilling to reveal his Welsh origins he disguised his accent and was taken for a Cockney.

There is a patronizing aspect, too, in his view of the Salvation Army hostel where he at first stayed in Montreal – all his life he was prejudiced against the Salvation Army. He arrived expecting it to be a place recommended to him, Joe Beef's Saloon, but was shocked to find it had metamorphosed into a kind of mission hall. However, he freely acknowledged that it gave good value for money, at fifteen cents a night for a bed and with a clean restaurant offering a good beef stew. Here he fell in with another man of the road, who told him that the American roads were now overcrowded and 'nearly played out' for beggars. Canada was not overrun in the same way and Canadians were warmer-hearted, he was informed. Lodging-houses were better run and cleaner. One such place over the border, visited by Davies, had insisted on an identification card for every resident, with house rules printed on the back: no person under the influence of liquor to be admitted; all residents to saw a fixed amount of timber to provide hot water for meals and a bath; no talking after 10 p.m. Needless to say, such regulations were not popular with the hoboes.

Davies waited three weeks for the snows to melt before he could start out to railride and beg his way to Winnipeg, more than two thousand miles to the west, teaming up with a former cattleman he had met years before on a ship from Baltimore to Glasgow. This was Three-Fingered Jack, who had lost the other two digits on his hand working at a cotton mill and now lived by his wits. The journey proved slow, but 'day after day I was certainly getting a little nearer to the gold of Klondyke'.

Railriding was a popular and traditional way of travelling for North American tramps, albeit a highly dangerous one. Trains and tramps were made for each other: a free mode of travel, plenty of hiding places on board, the possibility of covering enormous distances without detection. The freeriders might hide in an empty boxcar or squeeze on the bumpers between the carriages. More often they rode on top of carriages or underneath ('riding the rods'). With luck an intrepid man could catch hold of a board called a 'tramp's ticket' and lie full length a few inches above the rails. The huge gleaming locomotives, pulling ten or twelve coaches, moved fairly slowly and exercised a fascination for tramps.

Jack London in *The Road* gives an account of a not uncommon fate suffered by such a traveller:

The shack [brakeman] . . . fastens the coupling pin to the bell-cord, drops the former down between the platforms, and plays out the latter. The coupling-pin strikes the ties between the rails, rebounds against the bottom of the car, and again strikes the ties. The shack plays it back and forth, giving his weapon opportunity for every variety of impact and rebound. Every blow of the flying coupling pin is freighted with death, and at sixty miles an hour it beats a veritable tattoo of death. The next day the remains of that tramp are gathered up along the right of way; and a line in the local paper mentions the unknown man, undoubtedly a tramp, assumedly drunk, who had probably fallen asleep on the track.[5]

The shacks used every ruse they knew to dislodge their hated unofficial passengers. In the 1890s it was estimated, incredibly, that as many as five thousand tramps a year suffered death or injury on the railroads of North America. Many lost limbs, died from extreme heat or cold or simply fell from their precarious hiding places. Legend had it that some rail companies maintained mass graves for the disposal of unnamed tramps' bodies.

Although he wrote about his exploits fairly nonchalantly, Davies reckoned that riding the rods was one of the most dangerous experiences he ever had. As a last resort a tramp might stretch his body under a coach, on a narrow board four inches wide, fixed to two iron rods. There he would be unreachable when the train was moving. Sometimes he had to improvise a board; sometimes he would fall asleep; sometimes the rods might break. If this happened 'he must then fall and be cut to pieces'.

Keen brakesmen might watch a train pull out in the hope of spotting a freerider or else pursue the train, throwing stones under it. 'He is in a shaky position, without being helped to fall by a blow on the head . . . What favours the tramp most of all is that these men cannot aim straight, because the train is on the move . . . This was one of my worst experiences, being stoned while riding the rods.' If the brakesmen tried to pull a man out from under a train they would get him caught in the wheels – such obvious murder that they seldom tried it.

Another hazard in freeriding was possible intimidation by large gangs of robber-beggars who worked the trains. 'The desperate methods of these men were so well known that tramps would often swarm together in one car . . . For all that, several dead men were found every week on this road.'

A film made in 1973, *The Emperor of the North*, graphically illustrates the enterprise and extreme danger of this way of life. It dramatizes a never-ending battle between the railroad guards and the freeriders, who boarded at night and worked their way from wagon to wagon to avoid detection by their enemies. 'Hoboes roamed the land, riding the rails in a desperate search for jobs. They became a breed apart, nomads who scorned the law and enforced their own.' Their main sources of income were stealing and gambling. The film opens with a violent death. A fanatical brakesman on the Eastern and Pacific Railway is portrayed as a villain without compunction who would rather see men killed than scrounging a ride on his train. Davies confirms this brutality: 'It is nothing unusual in some parts to find a man, always a stranger, lying dead on the track.' The heroes of the film survive by their wits, dodging between coaches, hiding in a wagon-load of chickens, leaping off a train when it stops for fuel or water, rejoining it later when it is travelling at speed. What seems sensational to modern cinema-goers is borne out by contemporary accounts. Tim Cresswell in *The Tramp in America* quotes the moving words of an anonymous hobo who wrote:

> Inside the passengers sat, warm and soft on the upholstered seats, or lay sleeping in their berths. And on the prow of the giant land-ship stood three muffled figures, shivering but dauntless, carried on – through bitter smoke and cold and turmoil, danger of arrest or of beating – towards the harvest jobs that would earn them sustenance for a short space.[6]

Vagrancy laws, based on British models, were designed to make life as difficult as possible for railriders, and many ended up in gaol. Broadly speaking, the Canadian definition of a tramp was a man (rarely a woman) of no fixed abode and usually no employment. But the typical Canadian attitude to them was more sympathetic than that in the USA or Britain. Even as late as the 1920s 'hopping' trains was still a popular form of free travel, in spite of armed guards carrying out random patrols of the trains. And generous local citizens sometimes ran soup kitchens at the stations.

It was this vulnerable fraternity, the railriders, that Davies and Three-Fingered Jack joined in March 1899. They knew what they were doing. Even so the climate, the time of year and the immense distances they planned to cover must have given them pause for thought.

Given his experiences in the USA during the previous five years, Davies's haste to reach the frozen north is puzzling. Certainly he was not motivated by sheer greed for gold and probably not by an urgent hunger for yet more adventure. His hope to reach the Yukon and scrape a living there (quite literally) was unrealistic. After five years on the road in the USA he can hardly have been unaware of the hardships lying ahead. He may have felt that life had still something unexpected to offer him, even subconsciously hoped to find some God-given inspiration for writing. His own explanation is that he was seduced by the hyperbole of newspaper travel advertisements.

He records that he and Three-Fingered Jack 'loafed all day' at warm railway stations, where food was easy to come by and in the evening scrounged a night's shelter in the local gaols. On one occasion the scheme went wrong. Davies and his companion arrived at an unnamed town where a double execution was to take place next day and accommodation everywhere was at a premium. After refusing to move on, the two were quartered in a cell and eyed with much suspicion by the police. Davies's razor, penknife, comb, tobacco and pipe were taken from him, but much to his relief his small hoard of money in a money-belt was not spotted. It is worth noting that however hard pressed he was financially, and he had used up much of his £44 by this time, he somehow always managed to supply himself with (or scrounge) tobacco. A pipe was his lifelong companion, in times of leisure or equally in times of stress.

After a week Davies and Jack reached Ottawa, still deep in snow, and jumped on a freight train. This turned out to be too slow to satisfy their impatience to reach the goldfields, so they left it at a town called

Renfrew to wait for a fast overnight passenger train. And this impatience led to a happening which changed the whole course of Davies's life.

Renfrew, named by early settlers after their home place in Scotland just outside Glasgow, is a town on the river Ottawa. Until the St Lawrence was opened up for navigation in winter, and railroads followed the valley, the Ottawa river was the main highway westwards from Montreal and therefore towards the goldfields. Renfrew County is a mainly rural area stretching from the outskirts of Ottawa to the edge of the historic Algonquin Park, and the town of Renfrew, one of the larger communities at that time between Ottawa and Winnipeg, straddles the river. Renfrew County in the twenty-first century has a mayor (with the title of warden) and seventeen townships.[7] Towards the end of the nineteenth century it was a backwoods town, largely cut off in winter and dependent on the railroad for all its outside links. In March, when Davies reached Renfrew, it would have been snowbound for six months.

A hundred years since Davies's involuntary stay Renfrew is very much a tourist town. To visitors Renfrew is best known for Champlain Lookout, a vantage point above the town looking down on a dramatic stretch of whitewater rapids. It also has a large modern hospital, the Victoria Hospital, opened in 1897.

Here on 20 March 1899 Davies and Three Fingered Jack loitered in a warm waiting-room for an overnight train due to reach Winnipeg next day. From there they would travel to Vancouver and then north to the Klondike: a journey of several thousand miles which they hoped to cover in two or three weeks.

Twenty minutes before the express was due they took up positions in a dark part of the station where they could see the train but where waiting passengers could not see them. At the back of the passenger coaches was a baggage car, and the two free-riders planned to leap on the step of this car once the train had started moving again – by which time they reckoned it unlikely the train would be stopped to put them off. There they could ride undetected till the next station, fifty miles on. Davies does not suggest in any of his later writing that he had a presentiment of danger or any sense that Three-Fingered Jack was not the best choice of travelling companion.

The scheme turned almost immediately to disaster. The train set off faster than they had expected; Davies let Three Fingered Jack have the advantage of jumping first, expecting him to move immediately out of the way. For whatever reason Jack lingered on the step, not making room for Davies until the train had gathered speed. By then it was too late to jump on to the step. Davies clung to the bar and was dragged some distance through the snow before he let go and fell heavily on to the line. The wheel went over his right leg.

In his own words: 'I attempted to stand, but found that something had happened to prevent me from doing this . . . I then began to examine myself, and found that my right foot was severed from the ankle.' Since he felt no pain he feared at first there might be other injuries. Davies shouted for help to a man passing, who was scared and ran away. After a while a workman arrived, with others, and Davies was carried to the station and then by sleigh a mile or so through the snow to the Victoria Hospital, where two operations were carried out to amputate first his lower leg and then his leg below the knee.

One of the most remarkable parts of his *Autobiography* at this point narrates that while he was waiting to be taken to hospital he quietly smoked his pipe – a cause of much amazement to bystanders.

Whether Three-Fingered Jack did not realize he was making it impossible for Davies to jump the train, whether his disability slowed him or whether for his own advantage he deliberately delayed moving off the step is open to doubt. In the tricky circumstances of boarding a moving train without being spotted, more especially if two men attempt to do so, the chances of disaster are pretty high. Davies never publicly blamed Jack, but he must have reflected often on his lack of cooperation. Jack is never mentioned again by Davies.

A detailed account of what had happened to him appeared on 24 March in the *Renfrew Mercury*, a local weekly paper established in 1871 and still going strong.[8] A letter to the paper in 2001 seeking descendants of those who helped Davies at the time or who had family knowledge of the accident, elicited two responses: an executive assistant at the hospital, who mentioned that its centenary in 1997 had been marked by a book, and one from the author of *Renfrew Victoria Hospital, 1897–1997*. This was Carol Bennett McCuaig, who had also published a book about Canada's links with Wales, *In Search of the Red*

Dragon.[9] Davies is mentioned in both books, and a further link is that her grandfather by marriage was one of many compassionate local people who visited Davies in the hospital. So his name lives on in Renfrew.

In 1897 the *Mercury* had publicized a scheme to build a hospital marking Queen Victoria's Diamond Jubilee, to be called the Jubilee or Victoria Hospital. Within a year a twelve-bed two-storey hospital was built, costing a little over three thousand dollars. Much of the money was raised by public subscription. Problems of water supply and roadway approach were solved by public demand. The first patient, a domestic servant with diphtheria, was admitted in March 1898. The original matron (or lady superintendent), Mrs James Bromley, was not qualified but she had nursing experience. The first trained matron did not arrive from Toronto till 1901. In its first two years the Victoria Hospital had twenty-nine patients, and Davies was one of the earliest. If his rail accident had happened a year earlier there would have been no hospital facilities nearer than Toronto, and the likelihood is that he would not have survived.[10]

The *Mercury* in March 1899 reported that the local hospital, small and recently opened, had a patient 'once again'. This was a young man, 'not too badly dressed', three weeks out from the Old Country. He and a man with a maimed hand had hung about the Canadian Pacific Railway station, looking out for a chance of a free ride until the evening express pulled in. Because the older man was slow in boarding, owing to his deformed hand, the other one 'missed his grasp, and was flung under the wheels'. The newspaper reported that he lay in the snow for a while until he was heard calling by a railway workman, Mr James Galvin, who organized his lifting to the station and then to Victoria Hospital. Meanwhile the stationmaster was sent for. The injured man handed over his razor, knife and $143 sewn into his clothes, admitting that he could have paid his fare but wanted to save the money. Two local doctors, Connolly and Murphy, attended on the spot to his crushed foot, but at the hospital it was deemed necessary to amputate it at the ankle. According to the *Mercury*, 'Chloroform was administered, but throughout Davies exhibited such fortitude that Dr Connolly remarked that it was easy to understand how Britishers won victories, if they were made up of such stuff as he was.'

Dr Bernard Connolly, a Toronto man, practised at Renfrew from 1896 till 1913 and held many voluntary offices in the town. At one time he stood unsuccessfully for the provincial parliament. Dr Stephen Murphy, a local man, qualified as a doctor after some years of teaching classics and practised medicine in Renfrew until 1938. There is not much doubt that Davies owed his life to these two.

The *Mercury* also reported that Davies said that he was one of many British people who had been driven 'nearly crazy by the flaming advertisements of the mine promoting companies, who exhibit large gilded nuggets as examples of what are picked up in the Klondike'.

Although a second operation was needed to amputate his leg below the knee, in *The Adventures of Johnny Walker, Tramp,* Davies refers unemotionally to this momentous happening in his life. 'I decided to try my fortune in Canada, and booked a passage . . . But, as I have explained elsewhere, I lost my foot, which I left buried in Ontario, and returned to London. I was very poor after this, and was soon living in the slums.'

He spent five weeks in the Victoria Hospital, occupying one of the twelve beds: it had been planned as a general and an isolation hospital, but it opened first for contagious diseases and was ill equipped for surgical care. Medical treatment was not free, so it must be assumed generous Renfrewers funded his stay in hospital, more especially as patients were still a rarity. Carol McCuaig wrote that rates for the infectious diseases hospital were fixed at fifty cents a day, less if the patient was cared for by his or her relatives. This included the meals of the patients. Nurses there received no more than $1.25 a day.

The kindness and generosity of local people who visited him prompted Davies to write a letter of thanks to the paper, dated 1 May 1899. 'I soon found there was more pity in Renfrew than the most hopeful could expect . . . I must certainly thank the Creator of all things for picking out such a good spot in the universe . . . I consider myself to be a most lucky dog; I am really proud in having made so many friends.'[11]

Evidently the British patient was a considerable novelty and interest for local do-gooders. In fact he was invited to make his home in

Renfrew, and local people showered him with gifts, including some oddly chosen reading matter with such titles as *Little Billie's Button*. (Certainly Canada at the turn of the century had few writers of international standing, but Davies might then have discovered Stephen Leacock's humorous fiction or the poet Charles Roberts.) He had many visitors, complete strangers, who brought fruit and other treats for him. The matron's dog acted as look-out on the drive and gave audible warning of the approach of visitors. 'When it was known that I was convalescent this dog was kept so busy barking that his sharp clear voice became hoarse with exertion.'[12]

The novelty of having a seriously ill patient in their new hospital, and a non-Canadian at that, clearly moved the people of Renfrew. When he was told that a second operation was necessary Davies stoically contemplated his possible death. He was asked if he had a last message for his family, and a clergyman was in attendance. Indeed his life was in danger for three days, but within a week he was fully out of danger. After six weeks he was well enough to travel back to Montreal and then to Wales, although it is not entirely clear whether his family sent his fare or if friends clubbed together to finance his return home. The matron, Mrs Bromley, kissed him goodbye, and Davies confesses he could not speak for emotion – unusual in him.

He did not easily forget Renfrew or Canada; they figure in several of his prose writings. Later in life he said he had read in hospital an article about Robert Burns that inspired him to try to become a professional writer. It is intriguing to think that he may have decided on a literary course when he was in Renfrew Victoria Hospital. Certainly he had to face the fact that it would no longer be possible for him to live the life of an itinerant or one involving heavy physical labour. He had no wish to go back to picture-framing, for which he was qualified, and no capital to acquire a bookshop – something that had long appealed to him. Circumstances seemed to be pushing him towards the writing career which had always been at the back of his mind, although it was to be nearly a decade before he had any success. Losing his leg was a terrible price to pay, but without the tragedy he might not have turned to writing professionally.

Canada matured and sobered Davies. It also seemed that his wandering lifestyle had been arbitrarily ended. He admits to temporary depression, but the influence of a very lively one-legged man on board the homebound ship roused him from gloom, and his natural optimism reasserted itself. Soon after arriving at his mother's home in Newport in June he wrote off to London for a cheap wooden leg (costing twelve shillings and sixpence), discarded his crutches and with unrealistic optimism planned a new future for himself – as a poet.

Struggling in Middle England

If I cannot be free
To do such work as pleases me,
Near woodland pools and under trees,
You'll get no work at all; for I
Would rather live this life and die
A beggar or a thief, than be
A working slave with no days free.

– 'No Master'

BACK in Newport, the discovery that his grandmother's legacy had shrunk to eight shillings a week (with his not-very-bright brother's inheritance shrewdly placed in a trust fund) did not at first discourage Davies. Here he was, at twenty-nine, jobless, disabled, virtually incomeless. There was no such thing as disability benefit, and in any case, his injury had been sustained overseas. His disability ruled out many forms of manual labour, and he did not even consider returning to his old trade of picture-framing. He determined to live by his brains – by writing, as he had secretly longed to do since he had seen his article published in the *Monmouthshire Merlin*. He put together a small parcel of clothing and set off to earn his living in London.

The next few years of extreme poverty are described in detail in *The Autobiography of a Super-Tramp* but without much attention to historical and geographical context. His first stopping place was a working men's lodging-house near Blackfriars Bridge, across the river from St Paul's Cathedral, with accommodation provided for sixpence a night. The south bank of the Thames in turn-of-the-century London was fairly unsavoury. Dockland may have appealed to him because of its superficial resemblance to Newport Docks, but it was characterized by slums, cheap hostels and strong-smelling local industry – Crosse and Blackwell's pickle factory, Billingsgate fish market, breweries. Lodging-houses (or doss-houses, where virtually penniless men could stay for a few pence a night) were cheap enough but frequented by foul-mouthed and often aggressive characters, some of them Boer War veterans. His time in the USA had accustomed Davies to this sort of company in cheap doss-houses, but it was hardly conducive to writing poetry.

He moved on to Rowton House, one of a chain of respectable working men's hostels, in Newington Butts, near the Elephant and Castle and about three miles from the river. This was altogether different from the Blackfriars rooming-house. Rowton House also charged sixpence a night, but it offered sitting-rooms, baths and a well-stocked library. So here he settled for two years, determined to live frugally and not exceed his weekly income, naively expecting that it would not be too difficult to make a living as a poet.

This part of Edwardian London was noisy and colourful, dominated by horse-drawn cabs, street sellers, organ grinders, lamplighters and delivery drays – much the picture presented in Shaw's *Pygmalion*, better known later in its musical versions as *My Fair Lady*. *Pygmalion* was first performed in 1912, seven years after Davies became a published poet.

Rowton House suited Davies well. The residents were reasonably quiet, so that he could get on with his writing, and opposite was a leafy churchyard where he could study nature and seek inspiration. In a matter of weeks he produced his first serious effort, a drama in blank verse called *The Robber*, immediately rejected by the first theatre manager to whom he sent it. He was advised that giving the address Rowton House might prejudice possible promoters, so he headed his letters as from Churchyard Row. Another long poem, a kind of fable, met with no greater success.

As a journeyman poet Davies's next idea was to write a hundred sonnets, at the rate of five or six a day, then a tragedy, a comedy and some essays. No publisher was interested, except one who offered to publish a volume of poems if Davies put down £25, an unimaginable sum for a man living on eight shillings a week. Casting around for a way to raise the money, he hit on the notion of getting two thousand poems printed himself on single sheets (this cost 35 shillings which he managed with difficulty to save up) and selling the sheets from door to door. A witness described seeing him singing and reading his poems in the street. As usual he learned from experience, collecting only a penny. He was paid this to go away. No one wanted his poems.

Hearing of someone even worse off than himself (probably his feeble-minded brother Frank), Davies decided to help him from his small allowance and to look for even cheaper accommodation. This he found at a Salvation Army hostel in nearby Southwark, at rather less than half of what he was paying at Rowton House. The Ark in Southwark Street, near Blackfriars Bridge, was a terrible letdown ('I am sorry to say that I have nothing at all to say in its favour').[1] The food, the hygiene, the unpleasantly cramped sleeping quarters, the officers' attitude to the inmates; all to Davies were intolerable. His next enterprise was to consider applying for a pedlar's certificate to hawk pins, needles and buttons from door to door. One obstacle was his now nearly worn-out wooden leg; but a new one supplied by the Surgical Aid Society would solve the problem, if he could find fifteen sponsors to back him. The difficulty was that this was the summer holiday season (many to whom he wrote were away) and surgical aid was much in demand for returning Boer War veterans. It took much effort and some expenditure on tram fares to assemble the necessary letters. Eventually, in September 1902, Davies set out on his English tramping odyssey equipped with a new peg-leg, a box of haberdashery, a copy of Wordsworth and a pack on his back – 'the old spirit to wander seized me again'.

The English tramp was a different character from his American cousin. He had a long lineage, going back to the vagrants and vagabonds of Elizabethan England, and travelled mainly alone, pushing his possessions in a handcart or an old pram, equipped with sack, ancient mattress and a can for brewing tea. His overnight stops tended to be at workhouses. Davies stood out from this fraternity. He was scrupulously neat and clean and ready to sell his odds and ends when all else failed. He tramped what is now the A5, the old Roman Watling Street, well before the age of the car. Walking twenty-five miles from London to St Albans in today's traffic would be a hazardous business, but in 1902, in fine autumn weather, escaping from London on an open traffic-free road was pure joy.

St Albans, a busy cathedral town where drovers still brought their cattle long distances to market, reminded him of his days in Ohio as a cattleman. He slept one night on a common by moonlight, and the poem 'The Moon', one of his earliest successful ones, recalls that night:

> Though there are birds that sing this night
> With thy white beams across their throats,
> . . .
> Who worships thee till music fails
> Is greater than thy nightingales.

It is far from easy to imagine the problems that faced a one-legged tramp, however experienced, as he trudged from town to town, unsure where the next hand-out would come from or where to spend the next night. Davies admits that a tramp's life was not without danger, 'even in England', and he paints an unsavoury picture of thieving, heavy drinking and fights in common lodging-houses. He had his own devices for keeping his possessions safe if he had to leave them briefly. One was to offer a reward to the most villainous character on the premises for guarding his washing gear, cutlery and bedding. Fleas, lice and cockroaches were rife in some of the doss-houses, and it was common enough to sleep next to a lousy inmate.

In his writing Davies gives very little idea of the physical hardships and setbacks he met on the road as he travelled. There were days when he begged all day unsuccessfully or sold nothing. Weather problems are never mentioned. The general impression is of a philosophical traveller, not much troubled by angry rebuffs, crime or storms. He kept going at a remarkable pace, not lingering long anywhere. When a neighbourhood had been worked, that was it: time to move on, taking advice from others as to where the pickings would be most profitable and cheerfully getting to know any travelling companions he chanced on.

In *The Adventures of Johnny Walker, Tramp*, published in 1926 and so titled because 'there is a joke among tramps that they work for Johnny Walker, the road surveyor', Davies entertains with thumbnail sketches of characters he met on the road. They range from the aged pious traveller ('Put your trust in the Lord . . . I have begged for and fed scores of men in my life, knowing that a good deed will meet its reward at last') to the rogue who claimed to be a duke and was gaoled for stealing an axe and felling trees on an estate he alleged was rightfully his. There was Ferny, who carried a paper bag collecting rags, bottles and bones; if none were forthcoming he diversified as a seller of artificial flowers. And there was the handyman, anathema to other tramps, always quick to offer unskilled and unwanted help in barbering, boot repairs, patching clothes or similar routine tasks for which he would reluctantly be given a few pennies. However, Davies points out, the handyman had his uses as a hirer-out of useful tools to others.

He was impressed, as his readers must be, by the ingenuity of one Bony, who could feign an accident or an attempted suicide at the drop of a hat to extract money from a gullible passer-by. Equally quick-witted was the lawbreaking beggar confronted at one door by a uniformed policeman. His response was: 'I have had nothing to eat since yesterday, and I've come to tell you I don't want anything.' The policeman was amused enough to give him bread, cheese and a penny.

In *The Adventures of Johnny Walker, Tramp* Davies sets out a tramps' vocabulary, more comprehensive than elsewhere. His list includes:

Kennel – house;
16 farthings for a feather – a bed for fourpence;
Clobber – clothes;
Shackles – soup;
Chuck or scrand – food;
Rakes – combs;
Glims – spectacles;
Smuts – pictures;
Bouse or skimish – drink;
Needies – beggars;
Sky pilot – clergyman.

As he says, beggars' slang is to most people a foreign language. What would non-beggars make of 'I mouched at a red kennel and got a feather and some scrand for eight farthings'?[2]

Rarely, but unforgettably, Davies refers to the loneliness of a tramp's life, as in this passage from *The Adventures of Johnny Walker, Tramp*:

It is very pathetic on a Christmas morning to see seventy or eighty men in a common lodging house kitchen, and not six of them receive any greetings from the outside world. In one house, where the manager's charming little daughter received scores of letters and presents from friends, there were not ten out of ninety lodgers who received a single letter – on a Christmas morning! It was when I saw this that it came on me in full force to know what an isolated plague spot a common lodging house is.[3]

At Northampton, some forty miles on from St Albans, he abandoned the open road for a lodging-house to sort out his wares, only to find they had been ruined by rain. So he decided to move on as a straightforward beggar (a 'downrighter'), offering nothing for sale. By the time he reached Rugby, another twenty miles, he had run out of funds, but he had the luck to fall in with a red-headed man in rags enjoying a meal at the roadside. This kind-hearted character found it hard to believe that a one-legged man, a natural sympathy-rouser, had failed as a beggar. He gave Davies some food, bought him beer at the first pub they reached and introduced him to his style of begging – singing hymns so badly that people paid him to go away. Davies collected the pennies, at the rate of twopence a minute, and all went well until the redhead spotted a policeman in the distance. The two of them beat a hasty retreat, for begging in 1902 was a criminal offence. After this Davies and his new friend, now in funds, settled down in a Rugby lodging-house where on the day's proceeds they indulged in a good tea, a smoke and a newspaper. Here Davies learned another tramps' trick: to borrow someone's small child as a sympathy-jerker when begging. This was a device commonly used by female beggars, but it worked for men, too.

His next companion on the road to Coventry, twelve miles off, was a pedlar. When this man learned that Davies had a pedlar's licence he offered him half his wares, and they worked each side of the road. Four or five days in Coventry brought in more than nine shillings, around £30 at today's prices. When they parted company the pedlar insisted that Davies should stock up with £3 worth of laces, and so equipped he reached the city of Birmingham. Here he discovered an excellent library but a shortage of philanthropists.

Deciding that small towns and villages were a better bet than cities, he plodded south to Warwick and Stratford-upon-Avon. Stratford with all its Shakespearian resonances appealed greatly to Davies ('this enchanted place'), but he soon realized that he was selling barely enough to keep himself alive from day to day, let alone putting money by towards getting some poems printed. He therefore headed back towards London and the more affluent outer suburbs until 'I was satisfied that the workhouse was defeated for another night'. By now it was midwinter, his clothes were inadequate, his wooden leg was wearing out, he had no base to return to, and he was no nearer his ambition of 'a small room with a cosy fire . . . surrounded by books'.

So he set off for Newport, incredibly reaching the borders of Wales in under a week. This meant he was covering nearly twenty miles a day. Even if there was no stopping to beg or sell, it was a remarkable journey for a man with one leg. Even then, instead of making straight for Newport he arrived by a circuitous route, via Swansea, trudging over the Welsh hills in harsh weather, then finally treating himself to a three-week rest at his mother's house.

Soon after this Davies drew what he was entitled to from his grandmother's legacy and started back towards the Ark in Southwark. His plan was to catch a train to Bristol and walk from there on the Bath road, the old coaching road from Bath to London, in days before the domination of the lorry a pleasant enough route. This journey yielded him material for a good many essays in later years.

Later Days was not published until 1925, but it certainly mines that Edwardian trudge from Bristol to London. Davies's first discovery was that too many tramps trod this route for it to be profitable. He was dunned continually for money or tobacco, until he joined forces with an experienced beggar who acted as his guide. This extraordinary man conned the public into buying fake umbrellas which he manufactured from tree branches painted black. Men bought them at a shilling a time as joke presents for wives or girl-friends. Looking back over the years, Davies deplores the disappearance of this type of ingenious beggar, as opposed to the unimaginative workhouse tramp. He made many more friends than enemies among the sharp-witted fraternity of the road.

One unsavoury tramp on the Bath road touched him for a penny towards his bed and breakfast. After this Davies was obliged to spend the night expensively at a hotel, probably in Chippenham, as the town was otherwise full up for market day. He found the hotelier and his wife exceptionally friendly until next morning, when it transpired the unsavoury and uninvited tramp had called asking for him. Rather smugly, Davies 'expressed the deepest regret that I had been the cause of so unwelcome a visitor'. What, he pondered, caused him to be taken for a gentleman and others turned away? It seems not to have occurred to him that his educated speech might have been the explanation.

Crossing the Thames at Cookham he had the unpleasant experience (a rare cause of complaint for him) of having to pay a halfpenny at a tollbridge. However, this was to a degree compensated for by calling at a cottage where a well-spoken man gave him both food and money. They fell into conversation about Thoreau's philosophy, and Davies learned the man was disillusioned by his attempt to live Thoreau's simple life-style. He countered this by describing his own tolerable experiences in the USA, and the debate went on amicably. When he left Davies was showered with gifts of eggs, bread, cheese and apples. He was delighted at this success, but fellow beggars later remonstrated with him for not acquiring more of the contents of the cottage – such rich pickings.

Near Guildford in Surrey he fell in with a seventy-year-old beggar, the son of beggars, who had never worked, constantly quoted the Bible and insisted that he lived on folks' kindness. He had not stolen, had always gone out of his way to help others, and clearly believed his scrounging lifestyle was legitimate. Davies tells how they saw a man fall off his bicycle. His new acquaintance eagerly played the Good Samaritan, but to the old man's indignation the cyclist rode off without a word of thanks. The beggar had expected at least sixpence for his trouble.

This same beggar, when he heard that Davies was going eastwards, told him about a lodging-house where the landlord asked every new arrival his politics and sent packing those who gave the 'wrong' answer. The old man had told him: 'It does not matter in the least whether I am a Liberal or a Conservative. I am one of God's lambs.' So of course he got short shrift.

In Guildford Davies met a number of part-time beggars who carried with them a few odds and ends for sale. This caused him to reflect: 'It is a sure sign of a country's decline when beggars have to resort to carrying laces, pins, needles and self-made novelties . . . in England the downrighter is passing away.' All his life he continued to praise the 'true traveller' who relied for his income simply on begging. The word 'downrighter' seems to be a Davies neologism, based on tramping slang but absent from standard dictionaries. In old age, when he was living a settled and domesticated existence, he must have deplored even more the social loss caused by the decline in true tramps. To him tramps were not a blot on the landscape but a human and on the whole endearing aspect of society. (Soon after his death they became largely extinct courtesy of the benefits of the welfare state.) He was much intrigued by a tramping couple he met near Maidenhead on the Thames. He calls them Navy Jack and Portsmouth Nora. The woman supported them both by selling needlework, but he judged them 'not proper roadsters', for they would sometimes 'take a rattler' – go by train.

In Surrey Davies made a self-confessed fool of himself by boasting that he had successfully begged a shirt from a young woman, when it turned out she had palmed off a female petticoat on him. Some of the tales he tells against himself reveal a degree of naivety and unworldli-ness, as well as a belief in his own skills not shared by others. His disability caused him no embarrassment. He even tells a story of a beggar (whether himself or another is unclear) who was given a dead man's wooden leg by his widow.

In one of his more cynical moods he reports a conversation with an Anglo-American called Yank, considering the technical advantages of revolvers over razors as combat weapons – something he had learned in the USA at first hand. ('The razor is a sly ugly-looking weapon, but is far less dangerous than a knife, a poker or even a short heavy piece of wood, as it cannot pierce to the heart or brain.')

Together Davies and Yank, with a third companion called Ginger, descended on Oxford. They stayed first at a hostel kept by an Italian couple, which led him to remark that these immigrants (often former organ grinders) were more sympathetic to the men of the road than local landlords.

He tells a few anecdotes which one suspects have been somewhat embroidered. There is the tale of the house where the door was opened by a man who had just cut his throat. Davies fled in case he was arrested for murder. Elsewhere Ginger was rewarded with fourpence (enough for a night's bed) for killing a mouse.

Davies gives an entertaining account of the need for strangers to be wary when they arrive at unfamiliar lodgings. One of the commonest dodges practised by the old hands was to whip across to an unguarded frying-pan, add a small item of food to what was being cooked and declare total innocence that they had stolen another man's bacon. Soap, sugar and tea he found were always prime targets.

Somewhere during a week's walking between Uxbridge and Dartford (a distance that these days could be traversed in an hour along the M25) Davies was drawn into a debate on the relative life-expectancy of a white-collar worker and a labourer. He offers no personal opinion but ostensibly quotes his companion:

> Hard work does kill men, there is no doubt of that. The bus horse is a good instance of what hard work can do. In 1903 he is young, hardy, strong and shies; in 1904 he is old, worn, shaky and with no spirit; in 1905 he is cat's meat. Why, if donkeys were not stubborn, and did not refuse to hurry with heavy loads, they would not live very long.[4]

Some illuminating comments are made about the social hierarchy in the world of begging. Lowest in the scale come 'narks', men who do occasional paid work but not enough to live on: cattle drovers, hawkers, odd-job men. Davies castigates the narks for hogging the cutlery, the fire or the best place at table in lodgings. When not drunk they might be sneaking to the landlord and doing very nicely through bribes extracted from other residents. Between Oxford and Reading Davies met a sad individual, a man who had lost his job and also been robbed. He rather patronizingly gave him a penny. Arising from this comes some unexpected advice: to be successful a beggar 'must either whine or speak in a very quiet and gentle voice . . . Nothing takes a beggar more by surprise than [to be told] "You must speak out loud, because I am deaf."'

Davies had his *bêtes noires* on the road, and he made no secret of this. Among them were tramps for whom hygiene was not high on the agenda. He made a point of always being clean and well shaven, believing that this would impress the people he was telling his tales to.

He was piqued to discover that an unwashed vagrant in a ditch could earn more with his hard-luck story than he did. Workhouses were to be avoided, as lodgers in them would be expected to do menial tasks – usually stone-breaking on the roads. Davies held the view that work-house tramps were not genuine beggars and that they queered the pitch for non-workhouse tramps. Salvation Army evangelists or a nun collecting for charity also might 'spoil' a street for beggars. (It is diffi-cult to find a reason for his dislike of the Salvation Army, unless it was provoked by resentment at the Army's undoubted success in raising money in the street.)

Navvies – men working on railways or canals – were regarded with scorn by most tramps. Davies perceives them as always washing their clothes, making soup or drinking; they might resort to stealing apples or turnips. He accuses them of playing certain ancient tricks: palming off a fake gold ring or a dud razor on some unsuspecting customer; selling useless spectacles to old ladies; producing forged hard-luck let-ters presenting the beggar as having a wife and four children to support. Yet it seems that Davies rather admired the coolness of these deceptions.

Again and again in his prose writings Davies praises the kindness and generosity of prostitutes. 'Whatever may be said of a woman of that kind, it must be confessed that her sympathy for the poor and afflicted is most extraordinary.' In particular he noted how generous they were to homeless and disabled people. It was not difficult to find a bed for twopence, but who else would provide the money?[5]

On one occasion in London, after he became known as a writer, he bought a drink in a pub for a well-spoken 'woman of a certain kind' who took him back to her room, a room full of books. Davies was delighted to find she knew of his work, although he did not reveal his identity in case she thought he was wealthy. Before leaving he gave her a largish sum of money so that she could spend a few days reading without needing to look for clients. Was he being warm-hearted or remarkably naive?

In *Later Days* (1925) Davies set out his ideal baggage for two weeks on the road. It was minimal. In one pocket he stuffed pipe, matches and tobacco; in another a spare shirt; in a third pocket razor, comb, soap, needle and cotton, a nailbrush and a toothbrush. It went without saying that he always carried knife, money and notebook. At the end of a week he changed into the spare shirt and bought a new pair of socks. Presumably rather more changes were needed in hot weather.

Very occasionally Davies took a dislike to a tramp he met on the road. One such was a small aggressive 'bantam man' near Luton, someone who Davies thought had 'enough foreign blood in his veins to be dangerous'. But for the most part he praised their uncomplicated characters and lack of artifice. With a few exceptions he enjoyed their company wherever he met them, as he had in the USA. And he noted: 'Nature still keeps her interest for a man when he travels alone.' His Middle England journeys were to be almost his last experience of tramping alone.

Becoming a Published Writer

My mind can be a sailor, when
This body's still confined to land;
And turn these mortals into trees
That walk in Fleet Street or the Strand.
                                        – 'The Mind's Liberty'

IN 1903 Davies returned to London and settled for a while at a new address, the Farmhouse in the Marshalsea Road, Southwark, not far from Blackfriars Bridge. Marshalsea had literary antecedents: the original name referred to a medieval court presided over by a knight marshal. In Dickens's time the Marshalsea was a debtors' prison, as Davies may have known.[1]

The Farmhouse appealed to him, and it pleased him to put the address on his letters, knowing that most of his correspondents would never guess it was a common lodging-house. The building had a long history, although he probably was unaware of this. Originally part of the Duke of Suffolk's estate in the Tudor period, it had later belonged to Queen Anne as a working farmhouse. In its last phase the Farmhouse served as a doss-house for more than a hundred years, until in 1947 it was condemned by the London County Council as unfit for habitation and demolished. *The Times* newspaper carried a mock-obituary, mentioning that Charles Dickens had visited the Farmhouse and found inspiration thereabouts for characters in *Oliver Twist* and *The Old Curiosity Shop*. So it had literary connections before Davies moved in.

From here he eventually negotiated the printing of his first successful book of verse, *The Soul's Destroyer*, a collection of forty poems. The prevailing mood is one of unrelieved gloom, although a few nature poems – 'Lines to a Sparrow', 'The Cuckoo', 'Spring' – strike a lighter note. The destroyer of the soul, the curse of nations and the ruin of families is drink, something Davies knew a good deal about. Most movingly he draws on his doss-house experiences, as in 'The Lodging House Fire'. This is the outburst of a depressed and desperate man. The fire is perceived as representing both life and death, hypnotic in its glow, for thirty poor devils crouched around it. The poem reflects Davies's experiences at a time when his life had reached its lowest ebb. ('Pile on the coke, make fire, / Rouse its death-dealing glow; / Men are borne away / Ere they can know.') He writes of his birthday being spent asleep or killing time for twenty hours. During the other four he was kept awake solely by the fire. ('But all my day is waste, / I live a lukewarm four / And make a red coke fire / Poison the score.') It is hard not to read suicidal thoughts into this most self-analytical of all his poems.

Even the more lyrical ones in this collection are tinged with melancholy or allusions to madness. 'Autumn' shakes 'withered things' from 'his feeble hand and forehead wan'. 'Sleep' has power to make murder 'slink away', war to cease and armies pause. 'Love's Coming' counterpoints the loved one's voice with the frenzied singing of a mad bird.

Davies had had so many rebuffs in trying to find a publisher that in desperation he decided to pay for the printing of this collection himself. A firm of printers, Watts and Co. in Johnson's Court, Fleet Street (as he noticed, named after the great Samuel), agreed to run off 250 copies for him at the considerable cost of £19. He persuaded the trustees of his grandmother's estate to release the sum in advance and paid the printers on the spot. (The printers may have undertaken the work at least partly at their own expense, but Davies's own version of events denies this.[2]) He collected the 250 copies in March 1905 and sent off thirty copies to newspapers for review or to well-known people whose names he culled from *Who's Who*. The latter were asked to send him half a crown or return the book. A few paid up, and this was the modest beginning of his professional career as a writer.

The pale green paper cover announced:

THE SOUL'S DESTROYER
and Other Poems

by William H. Davies
of the Author, Farmhouse, Marshalsea Road, S.E.

Two Shillings and Sixpence

The years of extreme poverty, of heartbreaking rejection of his writings and tramping the roads of England, were over. Several of his review copies struck gold. Two newspapers hailed him as a Tramp-Poet; and one critic, St John Adcock of the *Daily Mail,* became a friend, interviewed him and wrote a feature for his paper which profiled Davies as an extraordinary literary find. In July 1905, under the headline 'A Cripple Poet: Realistic and Whimsical Word Pictures: Curious Life History', he wrote: 'Mr Davies has no pose, makes no excuses for himself, nor appeals for pity, but gives here, in a literary and ethical sense, the best and worst of himself . . . he has a personality and transfers it to his pages.'[3]

In *Later Days* Davies gives an amusing account of a visit he paid to the Adcock family home, bringing with him toys (one was a monkey on a stick) for the Adcock children – who turned out, to Davies's consternation, to be seventeen and eleven. He hid the toys, saying nothing, but told the story to their father later.[4]

In August 1905 he made contact with a literary agent, J.B. Pinker, who arranged the sale of some copies of *The Soul's Destroyer* for ten shillings and sixpence, over four times their original asking price. Publishers and reviewers now showed an interest, and the collection of poems was reprinted seven times. Davies was distinctly news as far as journalists were concerned – a novelty, a one-legged tramp who had worked on transatlantic cattle boats and now wrote lyric poems.

Davies spent that autumn and Christmas back in Newport, moving from one address to another without being able to settle. He returned to London early the following year and began, at the suggestion of friends, to plan the memoirs of his hobo days. Foremost among these friends was the poet Edward Thomas, seven years his junior. The two men had much in common: a Welsh boyhood, the struggle to gain acceptance as a poet and also to make ends meet. Thomas in fact had relatives in Newport. He also had a wife, Helen, and three young children to support, and he did so by seeking commissions as a journalist.

His positive review of *The Soul's Destroyer* in the *Daily Chronicle* led him to seek out Davies at the Farmhouse and get to know him. He wrote to a Welsh friend: 'Isn't Davies fine? I was terribly excited over the new book. Yeats wants him to "cultivate his instrument more", but Davies wouldn't know what the phrase meant.'[5]

Thomas did more than anyone else to promote Davies's work, to give him financial support and, from time to time, to offer a home to a homeless man. It was he who suggested that Davies turn his experiences to good account in a memoir. When Davies felt stifled and needed to escape to the country for a while, Thomas helped him to rent a cheap farm cottage only a mile or so from Else's Farm, the farmhouse tenanted by the Thomases near Sevenoaks in Kent. This had the attractive address of Stidulph's Cottage, Egg Pie Lane, The Weald, and Davies stayed here for two years. The two-room cottage on farm land was a congenial place to work, and there was always a welcome for him up the road from Helen Thomas and the children, who treated him as one of the family ('the poet at the bottom of the garden').

In January 1906 Thomas wrote in a letter to Gordon Bottomley that he had hoped to share a cottage with Davies but that he had been given notice to quit at the end of the week and that all he could then do for Davies was provide him with a train fare to London. He had given Davies copies of poems by Wordsworth, Cowper and Byron. Could Bottomley help with some more books, for 'I think he has immortal moments'?[6]

A year or two later an article about Davies by Thomas appeared in *The Odd Volume*, a collection written to raise money for the Booksellers' Benevolent Fund. Thomas regretted the possibility that Davies might owe his reputation to the sensational fact that he was a beggar and a poet; for, as he said, his poems were full of love for women and children, clouds, birds and animals. His poetry was pure lyric and pure poetry, without conscious artifice, but perhaps influenced in spirit by Blake and Wordsworth. His verse, Thomas noted, could descend to puerility or doggerel, but 'with inspired simplicity . . . he has rediscovered things that were discovered a hundred years ago, and by his sincerity reminds us how stale they had become to us . . . He remains a detached artist of unspotted sincerity.'[7]

Now Davies began work on his memoirs. Putting together an account of his life up to this point was not difficult, although many changes were made from the original draft, sometimes after reading passages aloud to the Thomases. Finding a publisher was another matter. A second edition of *The Soul's Destroyer*, drastically slimmed down, helped to pay the rent, and a small volume of *New Poems* was published by Elkin Mathews. Among these were 'The Forsaken Dead', 'A Blind

Child', 'The Jolly Tramp' (much less ebullient in winter) and a few more conventional flower poems. *New Poems* was dedicated to Helen and Edward Thomas, and Edward reviewed it under the heading 'A Poet of the People'.

Helen Thomas, in her *Times* memoir in 1963, spelled out how much they felt Davies to be one of the family: 'Davies was a short, stocky, dark man, rather Jewish looking and with a strong Welsh accent. He soon made himself at home with us and we all grew to love him for his keen appreciation of family life, his unaffected happy nature and his lively talk.'[8]

The Thomas children were especially fond of him – and intrigued by his wooden leg. One day they were out walking near their home at Steep in Hampshire when a country wagon overtook them. When Davies summoned the children out of the way one of the girls piped up: 'It would not matter if it ran over you, would it, sweet William, because you are made of wood!' Years later Myfanwy Thomas was not sure if it was she or Bronwen who was responsible for this utterance, but she remembered Davies coming to stay at Steep. 'I was not born till 1910, when the family had left Kent and were settled in Hampshire. By that time W.H.D. was in London, and my father saw him there often when he went to editors hoping for commissions to write reviews, country books, biographies and so on. I would only have seen W.H.D. very occasionally when he came to stay at Steep for a few days.' None the less she clearly recalled that Davies seemed to them an honorary uncle.[9]

John Moore records in his biography of Edward Thomas that Davies was invited to spend Christmas 1912 at Steep. Thomas wrote to the poet Gordon Bottomley: 'We expect Davies today sometime from Wales unless Swansea's defeat of the South Africans has been too much for him' – a reference to the national passion for rugby. Myfanwy Thomas recalled that her mother Helen recorded an anecdote of Davies needing to have his wooden leg temporarily replaced, without anyone knowing, while he was waiting for a new one. Edward designed a mysterious wooden object and fixed things with the village wheelwright, who sent in his bill: 'Five shillings for Curiosity Cricket Bat.' Thomas, who could ill afford even so small a sum, had a whip-round among friends to cover the cost.

Helen went on: 'In the evenings, over a pipe and a pint of beer, he told us of his life . . . He was not tough or callous or rough, and his manners were gentle and sensitive, especially to children and animals, and in dress and personal cleanliness he was fastidious. I never heard him swear or use a gross word.' It is difficult to equate the rough wanderer of Davies's tramping days with the gentle man known to the Thomases, yet he always had a strong affinity with children, the poor and with fellow poets.

Soon another benefactor came into the picture. George Bernard Shaw was one who had responded to Davies's appeal to buy a copy of *The Soul's Destroyer*. Indeed he had bought up eight copies and advised Davies to send them to other critics and men of influence. From an Adcock article he learned that Davies was a tramp living in a doss-house and trying to make an income from verse; that he had 'mislaid one of his feet somewhere on his trampings' and that his income was eight shillings a week. Shaw's friendly response encouraged the Welshman to send him the manuscript of his autobiography, and Shaw immediately offered to write a preface.[10]

This he did most handsomely. In around two thousand words he tells in his inimitable style how a collection of poems reached him from the Farmhouse, Kennington ('I was surprised to learn there was still a farmhouse left in Kennington'). An accompanying letter 'asked me very civilly if I required a half-crown book of verses, and if so, would I please send the author the half-crown; if not, would I return the book. This was attractively simple and sensible.' The preface continues by praising the poems ('a freedom from literary vulgarity') and outlining Davies's circumstances. Finally he thanks the poet for the privilege of reading his autobiography in manuscript and dubs him a super-tramp and 'a free knight of the highway'. Shaw sees himself as a trumpeter calling attention to a remarkable book. He did much more; he read the contract drawn up by Duckworth and Co., found it unsatisfactory and advised the author to go elsewhere, to A.C. Fifield. Shaw's wife was impressed sufficiently by Davies to finance the typesetting and printing of the autobiography. Reputedly she provided £60 for this.

Davies's choice of book title is interesting. By the end of the twentieth century the Latin *super* (literally, above) was being used to mean extra-large, wonderful (as in supermarket, supertanker) or just as a strong modifier ('That's super!'), but when Davies was writing it was chiefly a literal prefix, as in superscription. Nietzsche had conceived the *Ubermensch* or super-man (a man above others) in the 1880s. Then came Shaw's play *Man and Superman,* written five years before Davies's autobiography. There is no doubt that it was Shaw who proposed the switch from super-man to super-tramp. Indeed there is proof in a note added to an early manuscript copy: 'My Life, by William H. Davies, The Weald, Kent, 1908. Published as "The Autobiography of a Super-Tramp", the title being suggested by G. Bernard Shaw. W.H.D.' The manuscript was on lined notepaper wrapped in brown paper; later Davies made a practice of copying out his published poems in exercise books covered with brown paper, and a number of these have survived.

The Autobiography of a Super-Tramp came out in April 1908, and it was an instant success. In part this was due to St John Adcock's features in the *Daily Mail* and elsewhere; in part to its assiduous promotion by Edward Thomas and his friends; in part to Shaw's intriguing preface. But much was due to the laconic, unsensational style in which Davies narrated his hardships and extraordinary life as a hobo. For most readers it was a revelation that an educated lower-middle-class man could live in this way, let alone write so frankly about it. He neither dramatized nor underplayed his experiences. His style was not flamboyant, and he dealt with each adventure phlegmatically, so that no one incident stood out. Here was a new genre in modern writing, which critics compared to Defoe's picaresque novel *Moll Flanders* and Gay's *Beggars' Opera.* Thirty years later George Orwell would describe sharing the lives of the homeless in *Down and Out in Paris and London,* but for him it was a temporary excursion. Davies had lived as one of the homeless for a decade.

According to Sylvia Harlow's bibliography of Davies, the first few editions appeared as *The Autobiography of a Super-Tramp.* The hyphen was temporarily dropped in 1930, by which time it had become a classic, with more than 40,000 copies sold. Edward Thomas's glowing review in the *Daily Chronicle* was headlined 'The Poet and Mr Shaw'. The *Times Literary Supplement* had 'Duke and Tramp', and *New Age* carried a review by Arnold Bennett, writing under the pseudonym of

Jacob Tonson. Later he told Davies that he might identify Tonson as Bennett whenever he wished. In its first twenty years the autobiography was translated into Swedish, Braille, Gaelic, Russian and French.

In spite of his own hardship, his anxiety as to where the next week's housekeeping money would come from, Thomas was amazingly generous in praise of others. More than one critic has said that both Davies and Walter de la Mare owed their early recognition mainly to Thomas. The public success of his new book gave a higher profile also to Davies's verse, and more payments were promised. For these he could afford to wait 'owing to the kindness of a playwriter, an Irishman, as to whose mental qualification the world is divided, but whose heart is unquestionably great'. This may seem grudging gratitude, but that he genuinely appreciated the generosity of the Shaws can be seen from a passage in *Later Days*.

At his publisher's suggestion Davies visited the Shaws at their home in Adelphi Terrace to thank them. Shaw was out, but Mrs Shaw greeted him warmly. Minutes later she said: 'This is Mr Davies', and Davies was astonished to find that a tall bearded stranger had entered the room totally silently, materializing like a ghost. 'However the grip of his hand proved this was no illusion, and it was not long before he was saying how much we knew each other, through correspondence and mutual confidence.'[11] The friendship between Shaw and Davies was to endure, and so did the success of the autobiography. In the next ninety years it was reprinted more than fifty times. It became a standard school examination text, and extracts were repeatedly anthologized.

The early royalties enabled Davies to move to 45 London Road, Sevenoaks, in Kent, where he made new friends – among them the writer Edward Garnett. Some used to accompany him on walks in the Kentish countryside, finding him an agreeable companion, though frequently taciturn. W.L. Anckorn, of Dunton Green, interviewed for the *Sevenoaks Chronicle*, recalled Davies as 'a quaint-looking little man who stumped around Sevenoaks with a marked deformity of one leg . . . at times a somewhat solitary figure in the streets of the town. He had no use for small talk, and only to his closest friends would he talk about his work. He was in every way a lovable man.'[12] A photograph in the local paper shows 45 London Road as a handsome turn-of-the-century house sandwiched between two shops. This was home to the family of a local businessman, Henry Martin, and Davies lodged there for three years.

During this time he submitted a poem to the *Sevenoaks Chronicle* which was never published. It is written in Davies's unmistakable hand, on printed notepaper, headed: From William H. Davies, 45, London Road, Sevenoaks, with the title 'The Train' crossed out and 'Nature' substituted. It begins

> He lived a hermit for a year,
> His cottage had no other near
> . . .
> He listened for no loved one's feet,
> and yet his lonely life was sweet

and continues with a sketch of trains ('like lizards') passing his cottage at night, watched with pleasure by the solitary poet:

> That iron beast, as it drew near,
> When, barking hoarsely, it would come
> Faster and faster out of some
> Far kennel-town; or into a tunnel
> Dash, with smoke-clouds from its funnel.[13]

Davies plainly had no residual anxieties about trains despite the manner in which he had lost his leg, and he often commuted by train from Wales to London.

Another manuscript in a private collection which was written from 45 London Road is entitled 'How I Began' and dated 27 November (no year).[14] It begins: 'My first love was painting, and my subjects were ships.' As a sea captain his grandfather was highly critical of the technical detail in these paintings: 'When I painted a steamship with her smoke blowing south and her flags flying north, he was very sarcastic about the wind blowing both ways at the same time.' The manuscript continues with the stories of his writing his first poem and his twenty-mile journey to see Tintern Abbey by moonlight. He claims that during these years he was acting out the life of a poet. In this manuscript also appears the speculation that had he read more than six books during his wanderings across America he might one day have become a professor of poetry. As a tramp he had kept a notebook with a few scraps of original poems. This disappeared when he was sleeping in a barn full of hay in the wilds of Michigan, but one poem he remembered and much later published – 'To a Sparrow', written in a Boston park. Whimsically he reflected that although the Americans had defeated the British in the War of Independence, the common English sparrow (regarded in America as a pest) had reconquered the continent.

The rest of the manuscript goes on to recapitulate his fruitless struggles to get his work published in the years after his return from Canada. It ends ruefully: 'If I had tried the pages of magazines with my work, most likely I would have made something of a reputation three or four years before I did.'

The text's many spelling errors are intriguing: 'occured', 'reconquored', 'ancle'. It seems likely, in view of the references to journalism as the path to fame, that the piece was originally sent to a newspaper or magazine.[15] If other Davies manuscripts carried as many spelling errors publishers' editors must have had their work cut out to correct them all.

During his time in Sevenoaks Davies contributed an article, 'How It Feels To Be Out of Work', to the *English Review*. In fact the piece is more about the call of the road than about unemployment. 'In spring or summer, if a man cannot get work, he obeys the old lust to wander, even as a dog goes hunting. His hands begin to itch for something to do, and it is now a matter of chance whether he is to be a working man or a real beggar. So he takes to the road . . .' According to Davies, a man willing to work will take any job that turns up, from road-mending to hoeing potatoes, whereas real beggars will walk past laughing at the casual labourers. A genuine beggar sounds well spoken and accepts whatever he is offered – a lift, sixpence, a parcel of food, old clothes. 'He will now relish bread and cheese as he never relished the beefsteak and onions of his former days . . . I cannot imagine any better life on earth than to be free of all tasks and duties; free, morning and night, to rise and retire at one's leisure.'[16]

For the next few years he alternated between Fifield and Duckworth as his publishers, bringing out three more volumes of verse (*Nature Poems, Farewell to Poesy* and *Songs of Joy*) and a prose collection, *Beggars.*

Nature Poems and Others, published by Fifield at a shilling, included fifty poems, by no means all concerned with nature. The most familiar of these today are 'Robin Redbreast', 'In Days Gone By' and 'School's Out'. Edward Thomas and Arnold Bennett again gave him favourable notices, and the poems were well reviewed in the *The Bookman.* The new volume included extracts from glowing reviews of the *Autobiography.* The *Scotsman* had said: 'Open air literature has few, if any, books so delightful as this' while the *Observer* had described it as 'a book of extraordinary importance to the community.'

Davies now benefited from the expertise of an experienced literary agent, Frank Cazenove of the London Literary Agency. Cazenove sent his work to literary journals and negotiated publishing rights for him. Once again it was Edward Thomas who spoke for Davies in the right quarters. *Farewell to Poesy,* published in 1910, included the first appearance of 'The Kingfisher' and 'The Philosophical Beggar'. It was reviewed – or extracts from it were printed – in the *The Bookman,* the *Spectator* and *Country Life,* as well as in magazines which had reviewed Davies's earlier work.

Beggars came out in 1909 and attracted much attention by being seen as a sequel to the *Autobiography.* It was hailed as Book of the Week in *Country Life* and reviewed by Arthur Ransome in the *The Bookman.* It carried the first published photograph of Davies, showing him in relaxed mood lying in a field, with a walking stick and pipe. In later photographs the pipe seems almost a trademark. It may have given him reassurance or occupation for his hands, the constant companion of a rather shy man.

Beggars was a handsomely bound volume ('in grass-green ribbed morocco grain cloth') costing six shillings, but it was never reprinted. Several of the chapters referred to his American experiences, with sections dealing with American prisons, beggars' slang and female tramps (regarded by Davies and his associates as queering the pitch for their male equivalents). There is an account of a tramps' camp in Texas. The book broke new ground by discussing the injustice of a US law brought in to suppress vagrancy, as Davies seldom ventured into polemic in his writings.

In 1910 Simpkin, Marshall published a slim book, *The Odd Volume*, with articles and poems by several well-known authors in aid of the Book Trade Benevolent Fund. Edward Thomas contributed an article entitled 'William H. Davies, a Note':

> There have been policeman and postman poets and so on, who were remarkable only for the unlikely combination of professions; and it would be a pity if Mr Davies continued to owe his reputation to the fact that he is a beggar and a poet . . . The poet in him is enough to diminish almost to oblivion the superficial trappings of the tramp or beggar. In his poetry there is nothing that would have been expected from his other profession . . . Though he has suffered poverty and ignominy the melancholy of this age has not affected him . . . He is not troubled by any problems of economics or theology, though he wishes there were no starving men, miserable children, or misused animals.[17]

Edward Thomas praises Davies's lyrical purity, suggesting that he was influenced by the Elizabethans, Blake and Wordsworth. His two works of prose are 'perfectly himself', relating common – and uncommon– events in a style so simple that, according to Thomas, whether they are factual or not is unimportant. The same is true of Borrow's *Lavengro*, he argues. While conceding that at times Davies's poems could descend into puerility, naivety and even doggerel, Thomas felt that frequently 'it looks as if his mind sang itself into a verse, as snow melts into water'. Thomas's article must be viewed in the light of his affection for Davies. While he was reluctant to criticize his friend, he was well aware of his limitations. It was Thomas and Garnett who drew Davies into a small coterie of writers who met fortnightly at the Mont Blanc restaurant in Soho. John Moore, Edward Thomas's biographer, said that Thomas had few really close friends but that Davies was 'a sort of protégé, the poet at the bottom of the garden'.

In 1911 Duckworth published Davies's first novel, *A Weak Woman*, described as 'a Novel in Gothic'. It was never going to be a best-seller. The narrator is a painter, Harry Randall, who has two sisters: Maud, a daredevil with countless lovers, and Lucy, a quiet, homely type. Harry is conned by various London rogues, but he settles down in time and marries Helen Ransom, a good woman he meets helping a beggar on Hampstead Heath. They have a baby and live unadventurously until Maud erupts into their lives again as a married prostitute. From here onwards the story degenerates into melodrama with the murder of Maud by knifing in Harry's garden, his search for her murderer and the wildly improbable death of Maud's husband under a steam-roller.

There is a good deal of autobiographical material here, thinly disguised as fiction: the story of a false gold ring and the theft of some pavement art – confidence tricksters' ploys that Davies had come across in London; the kindness to beggars; parallels between Harry's struggle to be an artist and Davies's early writing efforts; an interest in prostitutes. Violence with knives was a topic that cropped up more than once in his essays, and the knife as a murder weapon figured in *The Autobiography of a Super-Tramp* and the later *Adventures of Johnny Walker*. The characterization throughout is poor, and the ending of the novel suggests a certain degree of desperation to finish it off. However, it sold a respectable number of copies, perhaps on the strength of public interest in *The Autobiography of a Super-Tramp*.

In February 1911 Davies was given a grant by the Royal Literary Fund, and a Civil List pension of £50 a year (worth somewhere in the region of £5,000 today). This was secured for him, in view of his disability, by Edward Thomas and other friends. W.H. Hudson and Joseph Conrad supported a petition to the government on his behalf. The 225-word document praised his poems as revealing ' rare spontaneous genius' and foresaw that he would rank in English literature alongside other self-taught isolated poets such as Thomas Chatterton, William Blake and John Clare. However, despite his standing in literary circles the sale of his books, the petitioners pointed out, had brought him an annual income no more than that of a daily labourer. He was still in his prime creatively, although in the fortieth year of a life of hardship and privation. The petitioners had heard of no more deserving case for a Civil List pension.

To this typed document Joseph Conrad added a signed note in his elegant hand: 'I associate myself with all my heart with the opinion that Mr W.H. Davies' poetical gift is of the finest and its expression enriching our literature worth deserving of recognition.'[18]

The Welshman preferred to think that his pension was in the personal gift of the Prime Minister, Herbert Asquith, whom he had met once or twice. The granting of the pension was reported in the *New York Times*; through successive editions of *The Autobiography of a Super-Tramp* Davies was now a name also in the USA.[19]

His profile was raised, too, by having some poems included in Edward Marsh's anthology *Georgian Poetry*. Marsh was a well-connected civil servant, secretary to Winston Churchill at the Admiralty and a patron of many poets. It was he who suggested the controversial label 'Georgian Poetry', rather arbitrarily, to cover a diverse range of verse published at intervals between 1911 and 1925. The project to bring such poems together was the joint brainchild of Marsh and Rupert Brooke, who was then staying indefinitely at Marsh's well-appointed West End flat. In the first anthology Davies had six poems, compared with five for Walter de la Mare and Wilfrid Gibson. (Rupert Brooke's biographer, Nigel Jones, queried the prominence given to Davies – 'a cracker-barrel sage.') By the time of the third anthology Davies was being classified as one of the older generation of the so-called Georgian poets, even though he did not fit easily into any obvious category.

The first volume had appeared with fanfares in 1912 and attracted much attention among the literati. Linked with this was the opening of Harold Monro's Poetry Bookshop in January 1913, a useful sales outlet and a venue for Davies and many of his newer friends: Edmund Blunden, A.E. Housman, Walter de la Mare and John Masefield. (Edward Thomas, Siegfried Sassoon and Rupert Brooke were also in the circle as of right.)

Davies had met Marsh at the high-profile opening of the Poetry Bookshop, and a few months later Marsh and Rupert Brooke had tea with him in Sevenoaks after visiting the Sussex studio of the sculptor Eric Gill. Davies asked Marsh if he could get D.H. Lawrence's autograph for him. Schoolboy-like, he was collecting signatures of the famous and rather admired Lawrence. As a result Marsh arranged for him to meet David Herbert and Frieda Lawrence in London, and they immediately struck up a rapport.

The Lawrences were staying with Cynthia and Herbert Asquith at Broadstairs, and Lawrence had heard that Davies was near by at

Sevenoaks. He wrote to Edward Marsh: 'I should like to meet him. He feels so nice in all his work.' He added an invitation, too, from Frieda, not yet his wife, and Marsh arranged for them to meet in London. The following month the Lawrences invited Davies to stay with them in Germany. After some hesitation, possibly because of financial embarrassment, he arranged to visit them at a later date in Italy, where some of his friends, the Georgian poets, would be staying. But by then Lawrence had changed his opinion of Davies's work. The invitation was not withdrawn, but neither was it pressed. Lawrence now seemed less enchanted with Davies's poetry. He wrote to Marsh: 'He's really like a linnet that's got just a wee little sweet song, but it only sings when it's wild. And he's made himself a tame bird . . . I think one ought to be downright cruel to him . . . Davies, your work is getting like Birmingham tinware.' Lawrence mocked his Welsh accent, his lack of poetic passion and his Sevenoaks base 'where he is rigged up like a rural poet'. In the event, Davies never went to Italy. He probably would have found himself out of his depth with the Lawrences.

Another leading writer who was less than enthusiastic about Davies at this time was Edmund Gosse. Edward Marsh, always concerned for the welfare of poets less well off than himself, urged Gosse to offer Davies some work as a reviewer, but Gosse rejected the idea. Anxious to persuade him, Marsh wrote:

> He's a dear little man, and rather comical. He has a high idea of his vocation as a poet, to which he considers he's sacrificed the last eight years of his life (he's 46). He thinks he'd have had much more fun as a tramp – and now he feels disconsolate and hopeless because after all his efforts he finds himself without the means to live 'the higher life' in moderate decency and comfort. He wants very much to marry and settle down in the country, and he doesn't like London . . . If he is allowed to have any talent at all it seems to me the clearest of all possible cases for a pension.

Gosse replied rather waspishly that he saw Davies as a 'moral and intellectual tramp' who had never learned 'the business of the art of writing'. Marsh defended Davies and had considerable influence in finally securing a pension for him. Later, during the war, he backed his hunch over the emerging work of the war poets Robert Graves and Siegfried Sassoon and ended his dispute with Gosse by mentioning that Davies was rather on his conscience – 'he ought to have respectable friends like me'. There is no doubt that Davies owed a great deal of his advancement as a poet, his social life and his improved financial status to Marsh's philanthopy.[20]

Between 1912 and 1917 five more small books of Davies verse reached the bookshops, and *The Autobiography of a Super-Tramp* was several times reprinted. Meanwhile he was getting even more of a foot in the social world of writers, largely through the Poetry Bookshop. The Thomases introduced him to members of the Dymock group of poets, so called because nine or ten of them owned or rented houses in the Dymock area, near Gloucester, for a few years from 1913. The American poet Robert Frost was the anchor man of the group. Davies was never regarded as one of them (Frost is reputed to have said that 'Davies stays too long and talks too much'), but he did visit occasionally, as did Rupert Brooke and John Drinkwater.

On a later occasion, in May 1914, Frost wrote to an American friend: 'No one doubts that Davies is a very considerable poet, in spite of several faults and flaws everywhere. But his conceit is enough to make you misjudge him – simply asinine. We have had a good deal of him at the house for the past week.' Frost also suggested some poets' rivalry between Davies and Wilfrid Gibson. One surmised that Davies was viewed as tiresome by some of the Dymock community.

Davies stayed with the Thomases at Old Fields at Leadington, a holiday home they were renting when war broke out, not far from the cottages of Robert Frost and Wilfrid Gibson. Edward Thomas and his son Mervyn cycled there from Hampshire; Helen Thomas and the girls followed by train. Walking and talking along fieldpaths in the unspoiled countryside was a favourite occupation with many of the Dymock poets, and Edward Thomas's recollection of walks with Robert Frost could equally well have referred to his many rambles with Davies:

> The sun used to shine while we two walked
> Slowly together, paused and started
> Again, and sometimes mused, sometimes talked
> As either pleased.

Eleanor Farjeon was a leading personality in the Dymock group, much devoted to Thomas, and she refers more than once to the close relationship between him and Davies in her 1958 memoir, *Edward Thomas: The Last Four Years.*[21]

By November 1914 the Thomases had moved back to Steep in Hampshire, where Edward more than once mentioned in letters that he had invited Davies down to discuss their work. Realizing how hard up the Thomas family was as the children grew older, Davies in 1914 made an effort to repay Thomas's kindness to him by urging Edward Garnett, as a government figure, to use his influence to obtain a Royal Literary Fund grant for Thomas. This Garnett succeeded in doing.

In the space of five years Davies's world had changed from that of a poet writing in a doss-house to an established man of letters hob-nobbing with the famous and no longer hard up for the price of a meal. The transformation had come about not through his poetry, as he would have preferred, but through the popularity of his memoirs and the practical help of good friends. For much of his life he had a knack of attracting the concern and material help of others: not so much pity for his disablement but, rather, affection for his endearing personality, being seen by many as the romantic Welsh underdog.

The long poem 'The Philosophical Beggar' casts a wry eye on the years when he was trying to establish himself:

> I knew Will Davies well; a beggar once,
> Till he went mad and started writing books
> . . .
> What ! Here's a poem by the poet-tramp . . .
> A truthful song, but will not pay his rent.

His income was certainly not huge, even for a single man in rented accommodation, but it kept him going, and he mined a rich vein of personal experience which was a resource for nearly all his writing.

Victorian Newport, *c.* 1893

Courtesy of Margot Clark

The ferryboat *The Welsh Prince*, on which Davies sailed as a boy with his grandfather

Collection of National Museums and Galleries of Wales, Cardiff

THE CHURCH HOUSE, PORTLAND STREET NEWPORT

The Church House Inn, Newport, where Davies was born, with the poet's head on the inn sign. Top: sketch of the building executed during Davies's lifetime

Right: Photograph of Davies *c.* 1908, at the time of publication of *The Autobiography of a Super-Tramp*

Courtesy of Rachel Sedgwick, Church House Inn

Painting of Davies by Augustus John, 1918

National Portrait Gallery Collection

Bronze head of Davies by Jacob Epstein, 1916

Newport Art Gallery; photograph National Portrait Gallery Collection

14 Great Russell Street, London, where Davies
lived from 1916 to 1921

From . . .

D807

WILLIAM H. DAVIES, 45, LONDON ROAD, SEVENOAKS.

~~The train~~ Nature

He lived a hermit for a year,
His cottage had no other near;
And there his summer days would spend,
With only Nature for his friend;
He listened for no loved one's feet —
And yet his lonely life was sweet.
The simplest things had then the power
To claim his care from hour to hour;
A small wild blossom was so fair
It filled him with a miser's care;
When near his gold that miser stands
And laughs with both his lips and hands.
Ah, what a joy to sit at night
And see the lighted trains in sight;
To see those trains like lizards glide
Through trees upon the dark hill-side;
Or, ere one came in sight, to hear
That iron beast, as it drew near,
When, barking hoarsely, it would come
Faster and faster out of some
Far kennel-town; or into a tunnel
Dash, with smoke-clouds from its funnel;
Or when, upon a misty night,
It in the distance with its light,
Passed like a comet in that space
Where late the hills had had their place.

Yours faithfully,

WILLIAM H. DAVIES.

Manuscript of unpublished poem by Davies, c. 1921

Courtesy of Sevenoaks Public Library

Painting of Davies by Sir William Nicholson, 1924

© Mrs Elizabeth Banks; National Portrait Gallery Collection

Davies in Stonehouse, Gloucestershire, c. 1932
Courtesy of Norman Phillips

Top and left: Davies and his wife Helen in Stonehouse, *c.* 1932. Above right: Davies and Helen at Yewdales, *c.* 1936

Courtesy of Norman Phillips

Davies in the doorway of Yewdales, 1936

Courtesy of Norman Phillips

W. H. DAVIES, Poet.
BORN AT NEWPORT Mon. 1871
DIED IN THIS HOUSE 1940
What is this life if full of care—
We have no time to stand and stare.

Top and above: Glendower,
Nailsworth, where Davies lived from
1937 until his death in 1940

Davies with his nephew, Noel Phillips,
c. 1936
Courtesy of Norman Phillips

Davies at the unveiling of the Church House Inn plaque in 1938; also in the photograph are the Mayor of Newport, Helen Davies (foreground to the right of the Mayor in dark hat and coat) and John Masefield (pictured in foreground to the left of Davies)

Courtesy of Rachel Sedgwick, Church House Inn

The Wixey family, who supplied prescriptions to Davies and his wife. Left to right: Nora, Louis, Marie, Alice, Peggy and Marjorie, *c.* 1920

Courtesy of Michael Flavell

Left to right from top: Louis Wixey, John Flavell, Peggy Wixey, Michael Flavell, Nora Flavell (née Wixey), Alice Wixey, Marjorie Wixey and, in foreground, Mary Flavell and Peter Flavell, *c.* 1942

Courtesy of Michael Flavell

Peter Flavell, Davies's heir and the grandson of Louis Wixey, who was aged about six when this picture was taken and when Davies's will was made, *c.* 1940

Courtesy of Peter Flavell and Matthew Page

The Leyhill prisoners' gold-medal-winning garden at the Chelsea Flower Show, 2003, illustrating the poem 'Leisure'

Courtesy of Jeff Goundrill

London Literary Lions

One or two poets would be invited to dinner, and when the dinner was over others would come in until there was a large party. At last I began to think I was being used as a public entertainer, and came to the conclusion that I could be better employed at home in writing new poems instead of reading old ones for the pleasure of others.

– Later Days

BY the outbreak of the First World War Davies had made something of a name for himself as a writer and a man about town. He had published seven collections of poems, the autobiography, a play and two books of semi-autobiographical essays and had contributed to a few magazines. Most of the journal offerings are single poems, but one was 'The Career of Hurdy Gurdy Joe', an illustrated short story published in *The Tramp* in 1910. He had been writing for this publication for about a year before turning his attention to the more prestigious *Westminster Gazette*.

Between 1911 and 1922 he had poems published in all five volumes of the influential anthology *Georgian Poetry*. These volumes promoted a cross-section of the country's best-known poets working in the years during and after the war. There were many critics of the so-called Georgian Group, some accusing the writers of sentimentality, but for nearly two decades their work sold well; this association with the group and Harold Monro's Poetry Bookshop in Bloomsbury combined to give Davies a high profile.

The years of the 1914–18 war were productive for Davies but also ones of turmoil. Not only his disability but also his age (he was forty-three when the war began) ruled out any form of military service. Yet he must have felt excluded when other authors he knew rushed to enlist. *Later Days*, not published until 1925, has some of his few prose references to the war. He complained bitterly about rationing, the rudeness of shopkeepers and the number of people experiencing nervous breakdowns.[1] He had felt himself to be on the verge of one, saying that he would often cross the road to avoid speaking to someone he knew – although this is hardly a convincing symptom when one considers that he must have encountered in London many victims of shellshock and other physical and mental traumas resulting from the conflict. Early in the war he briefly had a German girl-friend, with whom he debated their national characteristics, both claiming bulldog tenacity for their nation.

A letter he wrote in October 1916 to his American publishers Alfred Knopf makes clear the widespread wartime censorship. Davies mentioned that he had sent them a photograph which had been returned by the Censor. He asked the publishers to remind him to send another when the war was over. The official objection to his photograph is puzzling, unless it carried some secret information.[2]

One wartime incident is one of Davies's most quoted anecdotes. He imagined that he was being persecuted by a noisy London neighbour, a Belgian prostitute who loudly played the piano until the small hours every night. Davies complained to the police but was told in no uncertain terms that however tiresome he found her she was not breaking the law. One result of his persistent complaining was that the police started keeping an eye on him – not on her. He was naive enough to be astonished. After a particularly trying late-night rendition of the 'Marseillaise' next door Davies retaliated at 3.30 in the morning by playing 'The March of the Men of Harlech' four times in succession at top volume on his wind-up gramophone. The contest was repeated the next night, with six marches, and after this the Belgian woman gave up the battle.

Davies's other wartime anecdote from 1914 to 1918 is of a woman who stopped him in Hyde Park, pointed to the moon and asked whether it was an airship. On his nocturnal walks he noted how the lonely women in black had multiplied – 'I could not help judging life by them, looking on every soldier as a dead lover.'[3]

'The White Monster' reflects the bizarre sight of German Zeppelins cruising over London:

> Last night I saw the monster near; the big
> White monster that was like a lazy slug . . .
> I saw its big fat snout
> Turn straight towards my face . . .
> The great white monster slug that, even then,

Killed women, children and defenceless men . . .
Oh, it was strange to see a thing like jelly,
An ugly boneless thing all back and belly
Among the peaceful stars.

'In Time of War' also seems to allude to zeppelin raids: 'Where were you when this earth of ours / Shook terribly in the early hours?'

It would be wrong to think that because he did not write about it Davies was unmoved by the horrors of trench warfare. Two of his closest friends, Edward Thomas and Rupert Brooke, died during active service – Thomas killed in the trenches in 1917 and Rupert Brooke dying of septicaemia at sea off Greece in 1915 on his way to the Dardanelles.

In *Later Days* Davies makes unexpectedly hostile comments on Brooke's achievements as a poet: 'He was made to represent Literature in the Great War . . . if Rupert Brooke had not died, it is hardly likely that poets would have been asked to read [his] work to the public.' According to Davies, Brooke was not a major poet and there was little sign in his work that he would have become so. To admirers of 'The Great Lover' or 'If I Should Die' this smacks of professional jealousy. 'We must look on the death of Rupert Brooke as the passing away of a charming and gay young spirit; and to talk of a severe loss to English poetry is all sentimental cant and humbug,'[4] Davies commented. He partly softens the blow by praising Brooke's common sense, his sense of humour and boyish high spirits. But it is surprising to find how seriously Davies misjudged the work of a fine poet who was also his friend.

Cambridge Fellow or not, Brooke had seemed a kindred spirit. Edward Marsh in his introduction to Brooke's *Collected Poems* wrote: 'He [Brooke] began coming to London, going to plays and music halls, seeing pictures . . . and he made friends about this time with Edmund Gosse, Walter de la Mare, Wilfrid Gibson, W.H. Davies and many others.' Brooke planned what he called a Poet's Round, a circular walk visiting Davies at Sevenoaks, Belloc at King's Land, Gibson on the Gloucestershire border and Masefield and Chesterton in the Chilterns. ('Wouldn't it give one a queer idea of England?')[5]

It was at a breakfast party at Marsh's house that Brooke is alleged to have said: 'Davies did most of the talking during the main dish of kidneys and bacon, animatedly relating an adventure of his on the banks of the Mississippi which was not quite as enthralling as he thought it was.' Marsh, however, remained an invaluable friend to Davies. For instance in 1919 a dinner was held to celebrate the success of Marsh's *Collected Poems of Rupert Brooke*, introduced by a memoir that was virtually a biography. Marsh decided to use the royalties from this book to help other writers, such as Davies, and at the same time he bought Augustus John's sketch of Davies and presented it to the National Portrait Gallery. By the time he was fifty Davies had his portrait displayed in three major British art galleries, in London, Cardiff and Newport.[6]

Over breakfast at Marsh's flat Davies had met another war poet, Siegfried Sassoon. Sassoon was mesmerized by the sexual glamour of Brooke, a fellow guest, to the extent that he paid little attention to Davies, dismissing him as ingenuous and long-winded. In this period, leading up to the First World War, however, Davies was at his most productive poetically. He came to know Sassoon better, especially through the launching of the Georgian Poetry anthologies, but the contact did not survive the outbreak of war.[7]

In 1911 the publisher A.C. Fifield had brought out *Songs of Joy*, a collection by Davies of more than fifty poems. The best known of these today are 'Leisure', 'Sheep' ('When I was once in Baltimore'), 'Days That Have Been' – recalling his youth through a series of lyrical Welsh place names ('Can I forget the sweet days that have been / When poetry first began to warm my blood') and 'The Heap of Rags', a grimly realistic portrait of a mad beggar on the Thames Embankment. 'Days That Have Been' was one of Davies's favourite poems and one that he sometimes read in public; thus giving the lie to allegations that he was ashamed of his Welsh background. In fact he was proud of it but nervous that others might despise him for it.

Songs of Joy marked the first public appearance of 'Leisure', later to be so indelibly associated with Davies's name but not at first singled out by any critic for special mention. Although it was later included in most Davies collections, and in many anthologies, the reading public was slow to appreciate his deceptively simple world-view.

The following year he brought out another poetry collection,

Foliage, which included 'Francis Thompson' and 'Sweet Stay-at-Home'. Davies himself told the story of his first unaware encounter with the Edwardian poet Francis Thompson, meeting him in a cheap lodging-house, a silent stranger trying to read in the middle of the hubbub of the hostel. Thompson's life was dogged by ill health and poverty ; from these sprang his powerful poem 'The Hound of Heaven' ('I fled him down the ways, the labyrinthine ways'). The poet and critic Alice Meynell took him under her wing, and his circumstances improved. Years later Davies met Thompson and recognized that this was the lodging-house stranger; he was much distressed, when he learned the lonely poet's identity, that he had not been able to offer him some words of comfort.[8] The poem about Thompson, published in *Foliage,* reflects something of that wistfulness and his fellow feeling for him. To some extent he was writing about his own experience:

> Thy barque was helpless 'neath the sky,
> No pilot thought thee worth his pains
> To guide for love or money pains . . .
> . . . Some poets feign their wounds and scars;
> If they had known real suffering hours,
> They'd show, in place of Fancy's flowers,
> More of Imagination's stars.

'Sweet Stay-at-Home' is one of the few Davies poems that refers to travel – the Indian Ocean, the Northern Lights, cotton-picking Gospel-singers; this last is a surprisingly nostalgic reference to his time in the Deep South of the USA ('Thou hast not seen black fingers pick / White cotton when the bloom is thick, / Nor heard black throats in harmony . . . Thou hast not seen plains full of bloom / Where green things had such little room / They pleased the eye like fairer flowers'). He speaks to 'a simple maid' loved for her homely kindness, not for her knowledge. The poem brings together the romanticism of his youth and the realism of maturity.

The verse collections entitled *Foliage, Nature Poems* and *The Bird of Paradise* followed each other quickly in 1913 and 1914. Most were compilations of poems previously printed and now revised, but a few new ones appeared: 'Christmas' ('Christmas has come, let's eat and drink, / This is no time to sit and think . . . / This is no time to save, but spend, / To give for nothing, not to lend . . .') and 'A Great Time', with its often-quoted last verse, a particular favourite with Davies:

> A rainbow and a cuckoo's song
> May never come together again;
> May never come
> This side the tomb.

In the same volume appeared 'Rich Days', Davies's eulogy to the harvest of autumn. ('With mellow pears that cheat our teeth . . . With blue-black damsons, yellow plums . . . And woodnuts rich, to make us go / Into the loneliest lanes we know.')

Rhythms vary little from poem to poem, and the rhyme schemes are unfailingly regular. Some critics have gone so far as to label Davies's verses childlike; they have even been referred to as jingles. In so far as he wrote with the eye of a child the comment is legitimate, but it ignores the fact that he sifts his far more mature experience through that innocent eye. He also made frequent alterations to his manuscript texts, sometimes after showing them to other writers. They are not *jeux primitifs*.

During 1913 he spent a day in London once or twice a fortnight. He regularly met Edward Thomas and Ralph Hodgson, a poet who shared Davies's compassion for animals, and more than once lunched with Rupert Brooke and Walter de la Mare. In the essay 'The Camp' he sums up his impressions of 'Delamare': 'A very charming man . . . but every time I have met him, often at his own home, he has plied me with so many strange questions I cannot remember anything we have talked about.' He insists that anyone trying to interview de la Mare would become the interviewed. Davies gives an instance. On one occasion 'Delamare' asked him how he wrote his poems, to which Davies replied: 'First an idea comes to me.' De la Mare at once seized on this. 'What do you mean by an idea comes to you?' To which Davies replied, tongue in cheek, that when a topic presented itself he set it down at once in plain words and regular metre: a dig presumably at those whom he saw as more pretentious writers.[9]

These and other increasingly important social contacts, coinciding with a period when he felt his muse had deserted him, made him decide to leave Sevenoaks for London again. Self-consciousness was another factor; he was nervous about being seen with friends in local pubs: 'I know some rather good people round here; I wouldn't want them to see me doing that sort of thing!' He was a strange mixture, having a very high opinion of his own verse but notably lacking in social self-confidence. There could be several reasons for this: his unusually short stature, his physical disability, his unconventional family background, his history as a hobo, his Welsh accent. He never forgot that his writer and artist friends had for the most part public-school and university upbringings, very different from his own. Davies knew that he was no intellectual, but he never doubted his talent as a poet. What he now craved was respectability and distinguished friends.

In 1916 Alfred A. Knopf of New York published the *Collected Poems* first brought out by A.C. Fifield in London, and this included a frontispiece by William Rothenstein consisting of a pencil sketch of the poet's head. For the Fifield edition Davies wrote by hand this brief introduction: 'Note: This single-volume collection of what I believe to be my best pieces is published in response to a frequently expressed wish from the press and public. For permission to do this my thanks are due to the publishers of my separate volumes of poems – Mr A.C. Fifield, Mr Elkin Mathews, and Messrs. Methuen and Co. W.H.D.'

Meanwhile relations with his Sevenoaks landlady had became strained, so that this was another reason why Davies felt compelled to return to London. He found a series of rooms in the Bloomsbury area, finally settling early in 1916 at 14 Great Russell Street, near the British Museum, where the great and the famous came to visit him. However, he was still not financially secure, and in *Beggars* he tells of trudging the streets in a pair of socks improvised from torn strips from an old shirt. Nevertheless a boost to his self-esteem and solvency was the increase of his Civil List pension to £100 a year. Friends had spoken for him, even though Davies preferred to believe that it was the personal intervention of the Prime Minister, Herbert Asquith, that had secured the rise.

For eleven years, from their first meeting until Edward Thomas's death, Thomas remained Davies's closest friend and mentor. Indeed the entire family welcomed Davies into their home, and as a lonely bachelor he was grateful for this. One biographer said that they were like brothers, and Davies greatly valued Thomas's opinions on his writing. In May 1915, a few weeks before he volunteered for the Artists' Rifles, Thomas wrote to Eleanor Farjeon: 'You have a far finer and more beautiful poetry in you even than such men as de la Mare and Davies.'[10]

Thomas went to France as a lieutenant in January 1917 and was killed in April at the Battle of Arras, aged thirty-nine. Helen was left a widow with three children under twelve. Davies had been one of the last of the writers who haunted the Mont Blanc restaurant to say goodbye to him. They walked together along Charing Cross Road the evening before Thomas sailed for France, 'silently and neither of us feeling comfortable'.

Davies's memorial poem to his friend, 'Killed in Action', written in 1918, makes poignant reading.

> And we have known those days when we
> Would wait to hear the cuckoo first;
> When you and I, with thoughtful mind,
> Would help a bird to hide her nest
> For fear of other hands less kind.
>
> But thou, my friend, art lying dead;
> War, with its hell-born childishness,
> Has claimed thy life, with many more;
> The man that loved this England well,
> And never left it once before.

Davies kept in touch with Helen after her husband's death, and her article in *The Times* of 1963 gives an insight into her understanding of Davies's eccentricities. She wrote of her visits to him in Bloomsbury:

He was very much taken up by high society, and very much aware of himself as a poet. He had a flat over a grocer's shop in Great Russell Street, which was furnished by him as befitted a poet. He had heard that literary people burnt peat and he felt it incumbent on him to do the same . . . Edward suggested teasingly that he should burn his books and stack the slabs of peat on their edges in the bookshelves . . . At last the peat arrived and, having nowhere else to put it, he arranged the slabs as a sort of hearth-rug in front of the fireplace . . . Imagine his dismay when returning home one day he found a crowd outside the house, people running up and down the stairs, and smoke pouring out of the windows. A spark had set his peat alight; the whole street was interested and excited. This was the nightmare which Davies dreaded, this intrusion into his privacy, and that was the end of the peat. After that he was content with unpoetic coal.[11]

At the end of her *Times* article Helen paid her own tribute to the poet. 'To our children he was always Sweet William, and he remained our dear and delightful friend until Edward left for France. Davies paid homage to this friendship in a poem to Edward's memory.'

One of the authors he met at the Mont Blanc restaurant was Joseph Conrad, and Davies took up a casual invitation to stay at Conrad's place in Sussex. When he arrived he was somewhat put out to find a Polish visitor, a fellow countryman of Conrad's, staying at the same time. The Pole and Conrad held conversations in their native tongue which rather excluded Davies. During the visit he made a major gaffe by repeating a rumour he had heard, that Conrad held a Master's Certificate but had never in fact been in command of a seagoing ship. Conrad indignantly refuted this. The awkwardness was smoothed over when Conrad presented him with a copy of *Victory*. Davies privately dismissed this book, however, after reading it as 'sheer melodrama' – one of many instances of his tendency to write off the work of other writers with a sweeping generalization.[12]

Two other literary friends at this time were the young poet Richard Church, later to become a respected critic and editor, and a young American, Conrad Aiken, who had just arrived in England. (It was Conrad Aiken who wrote, in a 1951 letter, that Davies much enjoyed talking about sex – 'one gathered that there had been a lot of sex, and that of the lowest kind'; confirmation of Davies's rapport with prostitutes.) Later writing by Davies reveals that he felt he was establishing himself as a man of letters by encouraging younger writers. Davies was now forty-five, Richard Church about thirty and Aiken younger still. So to an extent he was building up the confidence he had always lacked.

In the case of Richard Church he developed an obsession that he was underweight and insisted on feeding him eggs once a week. In a radio interview in the 1960s Church remembered the Great Russell Street lodgings.[13] Davies, he said, was very suspicious of strangers. Church knocked at the door, but it was a long time before it was opened. 'Finally it was opened by a small man who stuttered with shyness.' By the door was a saucer of milk, Church supposed for a cat. Later he learned that the milk was an offering to passing rats, an animal Davies was scared of after his experiences of sleeping rough. His sentiment towards all animals made him reluctant to set traps.

Richard Church summed up Davies as 'an innocent with a peasant's shrewdness. You couldn't bamboozle him. Yet he had a great streak of kindness. There was genius hidden under his suspicious exterior.' In the radio interview Church recounted a version of the fracas between Davies and his piano-playing Belgian neighbour.

Literary friends who knew him in London often remarked that he saw himself as one of England's best poets, a view certainly not shared by all. One story circulated that he had heard that a Japanese student writing a thesis had identified H.G. Wells as the country's leading prose writer and Davies as its leading poet. His comment was that Wells was definitely not in that category. He also developed an irrational dislike of some fellow writers, among them John Masefield and Henry Newbolt. The basis for this is hard to detect, unless it was jealousy at their greater public standing. He once told Osbert Sitwell that Newbolt had been compared to an eagle but that he felt a vulture would be nearer the mark.

Sitwell was another writer who visited Davies at 14 Great Russell Street. In his autobiography *Noble Essences* he gives an account of meeting him first at wartime breakfast parties given by the artist Walter Sickert, where conversational topics ranged from the crimes of Jack the Ripper to the Impressionist movement in France. Another eminent artist Sitwell knew well was Nina Hamnett, who had undertaken several sketches of Davies and who had originally introduced him to the Sitwell family, Sacheverell, Osbert and Edith, over tea in her studio. According to Sitwell, Davies was not happy with one of

Nina's sketches because, although it was an excellent likeness, it portrayed him at a table with a bottle of port, which he felt was unhelpful to his image as an established poet. Davies was always most image-conscious. Hamnett told Sitwell it was Sickert who had paid for the port, not her.[14]

Whether Sitwell saw it as revealing or not, Davies loved meeting the famous at late-night parties, and he loved having his portrait painted (not least because he might afterwards be given a sketch or early version).

Sitwell sheds light on one of Davies's social peculiarities. He claims that soon after they met the poet called him Osbert but that he would not allow others to call him William until he had known them for some years. Moreover married women were never to be spoken to by their first names. Sitwell offers an explanation of this – 'his strong sense of propriety, coupled with an innate fear, I think, of husbands enraged at another man's familiarity with their wives'. On the other hand, Sitwell believed Davies to be almost blind to class distinctions, with a social independence bred in his unconventional childhood. He illustrates this with an anecdote linked to an evening of poetry reading organized by Violet Asquith. The room was filled, says Sitwell, with 'the perishable flower of Mayfair and the immortelle of Bloomsbury'. Afterwards Davies said to his hostess: 'It's been very successful, and you've had quite a nice lot of the neighbours in, too.' He was probably making a joke in his deadpan Welsh accent that Sitwell failed to recognize as such.[15]

Sitwell described in detail the poet's physical appearance, maintaining that it revealed much about him. He saw in him something dark and Spanish (the Celtic ancestry), long-faced yet rugged, with high cheekbones. He was short, broad-shouldered and vigorous-looking, walking with a slow rising and dipping movement caused by his wooden leg. In the Welsh accent Sitwell detected charm and also diffidence.

On the face of it the friendship between Davies and the Sitwells was an unlikely one. They were scions of a titled family, raised in a stately home – Renishaw Hall in Derbyshire – with other residences in London and Italy. They were cosmopolitans in every sense of the word and moved effortlessly in cultural circles, painted by the famous, all of them writers, patrons of music, ballet, theatre. Yet they were all three fond of Davies. It was Edith's habit to promote writers whom she felt to be deserving, and as early as 1920 she was running the Anglo-French Poetry Society, with readings by Davies and Mrs Arnold Bennett (a French professional poetry-reader). Another supporter of the short-lived Anglo-French Poetry Society was T.S. Eliot, whom Davies encountered although he never recorded their meetings. In general his distinguished literary friends crop up quite often in his prose writings. Where they are not mentioned – as in the case of Eliot and Lawrence – it can be assumed there was a coolness or that they had not made the fuss of him that others had.

Edith Sitwell was exceptionally fond of Davies. She invited him to her Bayswater salons, introduced him to the famous, visited him in his two rooms at Great Russell Street and generally adopted him as a deserving cause. More surprisingly, she lauded him as one of England's four leading poets in her book *Aspects of Modern Poetry*, which came out in 1934. This book had a cool reception, mainly because the critics questioned her literary judgement. She was scathing about Geoffrey Grigson, F.R. Leavis and Wyndham Lewis, while praising Gerald Manley Hopkins and her brother Sacheverell.

Osbert commended Davies's exceptionally small neat handwriting and remarked on his unworldliness in the matter of writing cheques or using the telephone. This was perhaps unsurprising; as a tramp he would not have engaged in either activity and tended to view both chequebooks and telephones with suspicion.

Max Beerbohm was another literary celebrity Davies met at this time, at a dinner party given by the artist William Nicholson. Davies's first impression was of a shy man 'who would go through life with his eyes on the ground, to give worms their right to cross his path'. He soon learned his mistake: Beerbohm, he decided, had a tongue as powerful as his pen. They clashed over an article written as an attack on Bernard Shaw. After dinner Beerbohm asked Davies how long he had known Shaw and was told fourteen or fifteen years. His response was: 'Oh dear, and has it been going on all this time?' which Davies touchily interpreted as suggesting that it was time Shaw forgot him.[16] Beerbohm evidently tried to mollify Davies but only made matters worse by explaining that he had merely meant that Shaw had lent a hand to help a lame dog over a stile. Davies, sensitive as ever, took this as a personal reference to his disability and would not be persuaded otherwise. This was permanently to sour their relationship, and the Welshman never had anything good to say about Beerbohm after this.

As well as mixing with some of the most important literary figures of the age Davies was now beginning to move in prestigious art circles, sitting for well-known artists and counting them as his friends. An early spotter of Davies's talent was Walter Sickert, who did several sketches of him. In *Later Days* Davies recalls a discussion during which the painter bemoaned the fact that artists could not get the government assistance available to writers and scientists. Davies's reaction was that artists who could command £5,000 a year had no need of state help, while writers, some existing on £50 a year, did. He somewhat illogically tried to compare the market value of a John painting and a Yeats poem. Sickert riposted by pointing out the expense of an artist's materials and studio – a poet needed only a small space and some ink to produce a work of genius. Soon after Davies saw a Sickert drawing in a shop priced at £15. Coveting it, he asked Sickert if it was genuine, and a deal was struck between them: each would give the other one of his works. Davies felt he had had much the better of the bargain and praised Sickert's generosity, charm and wit. For a time he joined Sickert at breakfast in his Soho studio, with one or two other friends, on Friday mornings, and Sickert was to draw several more sketches of him. This ended when the artist moved to France, but they remained friends.

The first portraitist he sat for regularly was William Rothenstein, visiting him at his Cotswold home and studio at Oakridge near Stroud. Rothenstein's 1916 delicate pencil sketch makes the poet appear fair rather than black-haired and gives him a less sensuous mouth than most impressions of him convey. Attention is focused on his eyes. The artist spent his mornings doing various views of a single tree, which fascinated Davies. In *Later Days* the poet admits that Rothenstein's 'large fat smile' as he painted had irritated him excessively, but the artist's smile in the evening, when he was with his three children, was 'a different thing altogether'. Another activity at night was listening to Rothenstein reading poems by the Indian poet Rabindranath Tagore, a friend who occasionally stayed at Oakridge. 'I offered a little criticism, but Rothenstein . . . still went on reading.'[17]

One explanation of his ambiguous attitude to Rothenstein lies in his claim that this was the only artist who painted his portrait but did not give him a copy. Davies always looked for a reward for his 'obligingness'. Some years later he wrote to Jonathan Cape, his publisher, referring to 'this trouble with Rothenstein'. Whatever the problem was, Davies castigated Rothenstein as 'very ungenerous, especially as I have sat to him for another portrait'.

A week or two after this he sent a brief message to Cape saying that he had been laid up with rheumatic gout and expected to be a prisoner for at least a week. In general he was scrupulous about meeting publishers' deadlines, but this tendency to rheumatism was to plague him at intervals for the rest of his life.

In the same year he met the sculptor Jacob Epstein, whose powerful bronze bust of him was created almost certainly in 1916. Davies records that a recruitment tribunal had considered whether Epstein should be called up (he was then thirty-seven), and he quotes the tribunal chairman: 'You have made a great name as a sculptor, and we are going to give you a chance now to make a name as a soldier.' These men who sat on tribunals, dealing with conscientious objectors as well as those claiming reserved occupations, were not only brutal but often ignorant men, Davies observes dismissively.

The story of Epstein's exemption from war service is a complicated one. He had hoped to be commissioned as an official war artist, but the War Office objected on the grounds that he was both American and Jewish. Conscription began early in 1916, and Epstein was due to be called up into the army in June. He set about pulling strings, and an influential American art collector cabled the War Office pleading for Epstein's exemption on the grounds that he was one of the two or three greatest living sculptors, with important work in hand. Others supported this, but Epstein's appeal against call-up was rejected three times. He was allowed three months to finish his work in progress (which almost certainly included the bronze of Davies). This appeal rejection caused a public outcry when it was reported in the press, and questions were asked in the House of Commons. In September Epstein was finally called up as a private in a Jewish infantry regiment and after training ordered to Mesopotamia. The result of this was a mental breakdown, but by 1918 the string-pulling had worked and Epstein was sent to France as a war artist.[18]

Davies draws back from commenting generally on Epstein's art, but he coveted the head of a baby priced at sixty guineas – far beyond his means –in a West End gallery. He characterized Epstein as a man deeply, almost obsessively suspicious of others, and this is confirmed by other writers. 'I got on very well with Epstein, as I always do with Jews, or for that matter anyone else. What he needed . . . was a good friend to tell him that he did not have as many enemies as he believed.' Davies was not always as tolerant as this.

The sittings took place at Epstein's studio in Guildford Street, Bloomsbury, and artist and sitter became good friends. The sculptor has captured the rugged Celticism of Davies's profile and his combination of boldness and anxiety. Many who knew him thought the bronze portrayed Davies's unusual features better than paintings of him, and he liked it well enough to have copies (given him by Epstein) or pictures of it displayed in his subsequent homes. However, legend has it that Davies's wife Helen strongly disliked the bust and refused to give house room to any copies of it. The bronze original was bought almost immediately for the town of Newport by Lord Tredegar, the industrialist and philanthropist whose ancestor fought at Balaclava, and given to Newport Art Gallery, where it still resides.

Possibly the best known – and oddest – portrait of the poet was painted in oils, probably in 1916, by Augustus John, a fellow Welshman. Davies called it 'the most astonishing portrait I have ever seen'. The history of this painting is rather remarkable. John wrote in his autobiography: 'I was eager to make a record of this little man of genius, with his fine features, dark complexion and high black toupet [*sic*]. He sat as one inspired, his hands clasped before him, his eyes focused, as it were, on Paradise, and his ears, it might be, intent on the song of an invisible bird.' (John was not the only acquaintance who thought that Davies's strange hairdo was a wig.[19]) The poet explained his rapt expression more prosaically. He had fixed his eyes on a glimmer of light which came through a curtain. After twenty minutes or so the light seemed closer and had increased in size. He surmised that he had half hypnotized himself by staring so fixedly, hence his mesmerized expression. He was roused by the sound of John knocking the ash out of his pipe; by then the light had vanished. Mesmerized or not, his expression is intense, and the high colour almost gives the impression that Davies was wearing make-up. His lips are a vivid red, while his quiff is brushed higher than usual and his hands are locked together anxiously. Perhaps deliberately the portrait romanticizes the poet.

The portrait was donated to the National Museum of Wales by a generous Cardiff collector of French paintings, Gwendoline Davies (no relation), who by 1916 had begun to collect work by Augustus John. In 1919 she bought the Davies portrait from the Chenil Gallery in London for £550, and she and her sister Margaret went on to give some two dozen Johns to the National Museum, where they hang now in a special gallery. Davies hangs next to a portrait of fellow Welsh poet Dylan Thomas.

In 1918 John did a drawing of Davies, based on the oil painting, which was exhibited by the Contemporary Arts Society at Zurich. The artist gave it to the poet as a present, and at first he had it in his room but later grew to dislike it as he felt it made him look comical. Sitting in the Café Royal in London one day he overheard a man say to another: 'That's Davies, the poet.' He was subsequently affronted when his companion identified him as the subject of a John portrait. 'I was not very well pleased to think I was only a John, and nothing more.'[20]

A close friend at the end of the war was the artist Sir William Nicholson who first introduced Davies to arts café society at the Café Royal. He loved being taken there and mixing with celebrities from every field, and he became friendly with Nicholson's wife and family, staying with them at Rottingdean in what had been Burne-Jones's house and going on picnics with the Nicholson children. Davies was impressed by Nicholson's inventiveness in devising practical jokes, although he never carried them out. One hare-brained scheme was to drop red powder into Trafalgar Square's fountains so that they would seem to spout blood. It was William Nicholson who became the most distinguished illustrator of Davies's books and produced for *The Hour of Magic* an almost surrealist drawing of the author asleep at a table. His delicate pen-and-ink sketches for the collection of poems include a cockerel, an owl, a woman nursing her baby, maypole-dancing, horse-ploughing and similar rural scenes. The first poem in the book is a popular one:

> Three things there are more beautiful
> Than any man could wish to see.
> The first it is a full-rigged ship,
> Sailing with all her sails set free.

(The other symbols of beauty are a windswept field of corn and a pregnant woman.)

Jonathan Cape brought out in 1922 a limited edition of *The Hour of Magic,* 110 copies numbered and signed by both author and artist, at 25 shillings. Eighty years later the market value of one of these copies had increased hundredfold. The book was well reviewed in the *Times Literary Supplement,* but the reviewer compared Davies somewhat unfavourably with John Masefield, Walter de la Mare and Laurence Binyon – which may go some way to explain his later animosity towards Masefield and de la Mare.[21]

Another artist of note who painted and befriended Davies was Laura Knight (later Dame Laura). She illustrated *The Song of Life* in 1920, and he stayed with her family near the beauty spot of Lamorna Cove in Cornwall. This visit led to his poem 'Lamorna Cove', identifying the poet with the place:

> I see at last our great Lamorna Cove
> Which, danced on by ten thousand silver feet,
> Has all those waves that run like little lambs.
> . . .
> And, like the wild gulls flashing in my sight,
> Each furious thought that's driving through my brain
> Screams in its fresh young wonder and delight.

Dame Laura in a radio interview recorded some personal memories of Davies. 'He was a tramp at heart really, suspicious of everybody and nervous of going into pubs because he didn't know whom he might meet. I think he was ashamed that his mother lived in a poor house and he couldn't afford to give her a home.' Dame Laura did a pencil drawing of Davies and said: 'No woman could refuse his big brown eyes with curly lashes – they took you by storm.'[22] Soon after this he stayed again with the Knights at their Cornish home, where 'his conformity didn't conform with ours'. She remembered, as many people did, his strange hairstyle – 'black bristles at the back, and in front like a cockatoo'. He brought four shirts to last for five weeks and the fifth week he rotated them in turn. Once they found him outside in the corridor brandishing his wooden leg, saying he was on the look-out for ghosts. To Dame Laura he was an entirely lovable eccentric.

Davies did not allow the war to curtail his literary output. Apart from his work in the various volumes of *Georgian Poetry*, between 1914 and 1918 he brought out five new verse collections and another collection of essays and poems about his tramping adventures a decade earlier. He called them 'going on the tramp'.

A Poet's Pilgrimage, published in 1918 by Andrew Melrose, focusing on his Welsh and central English journeys, includes the verse self-portrait allegedly written for a fellow walker between Caerphilly and Cardiff to prove that he was a poet:

> I am the poet, Davies, William . . .
> I am a man that lives to eat;
> I am a man that lives to drink.
> My face is large, my lips are thick,
> My skin is coarse and black almost;
> But the ugliest feature is my verse,
> Which proves my soul is black and lost.

In this collection more than anywhere Davies seems to feel at home in Wales. Of Chepstow Castle he writes: 'Those walls which were once so dangerous, being alive with armed men, were now used only by the birds that built nests in the crevices.'[23] But he is at his most lyrical in describing the countryside around Newport, which he knew so well, and its myths. He tells with a folk historian's voice the myth of Gutto Nyth Bran, the fastest runner ever known in South Wales, reputed to have run sixteen miles in less than sixteen minutes to fetch yeast for his mother to make bread; and he recycles the popular stories of Welsh bards, prophets and Wesleyan ministers. He brings to life the dramatic black hills of the Rhondda Valley, turned to green and gold by the evening light.

Even the names of Welsh pubs he stopped at have a ring: the Three Blackbirds, the Philanthropic Inn, the Ty-yn-y-Phll. After a brief stay in Newport to visit old friends he pressed on towards industrial South Wales, through Pontypool, Cwmbran, Cross Keys, Risca and Caerphilly ('so well known for its old castle and a certain good cheese') and on to the city of Cardiff, which evidently he had not seen before ('it was not too dark to see the fine public buildings erected there, and their size and magnificence made me think of London'). It is hard to believe that he was walking through some of the most industrialized areas in Britain. Save for a reference to slum housing or the blackened fleeces of local sheep, the urban landscape is not pictured.

Nowhere in his prose writings does Davies explain his choice of routes; he seldom comments on scenery or great tourist sights; he scarcely refers to the weather, to the traffic which must have troubled him on main roads – for there were already quite a few cars, buses and charabancs. His interest is focused on the people he meets on the road and on his varied overnight stops. Later, in verse, he makes good the omission as far as landscapes and seasons are concerned, but this was a man who at the time walked warily with his eyes on the road ahead, on the look-out for opportunities.

From Cardiff Davies took a train to Bristol and then to Chippenham, planning to walk from there towards London. This part of *A Poet's Pilgrimage* is chiefly memorable for the pen portraits of characters he met on the way: the gypsy woman with whom he shared a match to light both their pipes; the man tormented by lice. Now and then comes a vignette of natural history: the two cuckoos singing 'like a blacksmith's hammer and tongs, and playing seesaw with their voices'.

Women tramps intrigued him. 'Women are much better beggars than men. In the first place they are much better talkers, and in the second place they have more confidence, knowing the police are not likely to do any more than warn them.' A chance encounter with shabby woman in black led to a diatribe about workhouses, which

Davies found inexplicably amusing. As with prostitutes, he was far less shy among women beggars than with other females, although the more enterprising ones rather overawed him.

The Wiltshire and Berkshire essays are memorable not for the observation of landscape or farm buildings but more for the oddity of the characters he met on the way, ranging from a rag-and-bone philosopher to landed gentry driving donkey carts through Savernake Forest. Here and there a few nuggets of wisdom enliven the anecdotes. Davies notes that beggars despise navvies because they work so hard for their living, whereas navvies disparage beggars because they can live without working.[23]

Davies's tramping from Chepstow to Cardiff and from Bristol to Maidenhead seems to have yielded less colourful material than his transatlantic wanderings. It was less hazardous and a good deal more incident-free. Certain parallels can be drawn between his portrait of the open road in the early years of the twentieth century and George Borrow's *Lavengro* and *Romany Rye,* accounts of gypsies, rogues and adventurers in the mid nineteenth century. The label 'picaresque' has been attached to Borrow's semi-autobiographical novels, which do seem in some ways to foreshadow Davies's, but there is no evidence that the Welshman ever read Borrow.

In the years after the First World War Davies was invited now and then to dinner parties in Osbert and Sacheverell's sumptuous flat in Carlyle Square, where the dining-room, upholstered in blue and silver, 'resembled a grotto under the sea'. Osbert himself listed some of the great who sat around his marble dining-table; among them Arnold Bennett, Maurice Ravel, W.H. Davies, Virginia Woolf, Leonide Massine, George Gershwin and T.S. Eliot.

The Anglo-French Poetry Society, at which Davies read his poems aloud, had been formed in 1920, and around this time Osbert took Edith on her first visit to the poet in his one room in Great Russell Street. This was during the period of post-war rationing, and Davies amused Edith by offering her a cup of tea ('I shall be glad to give you one cup . . . but no more').[24] Davies was in the habit of walking from Bloomsbury to Bayswater to attend Edith's Saturday tea parties: he almost never took a bus or used the London Underground. One Saturday he arrived late, making the excuse that he had to make a detour because Oxford Street was full of police. Throughout his life he never overcame his suspicion of policemen.

In his autobiography Osbert tells his own version of Davies's Belgian-neighbour story. According to him the problem was eventually solved by the Sitwell brothers who lent him a metronome used by their sister when she was learning to play the piano. He could set this to tick, to infuriate his neighbour, even when he was out.

The Sitwells delighted Davies by taking him to the Chelsea Palace music-hall, and once the turns included some performing elephants. As Osbert, Sacheverell and Davies were walking back to Swan Walk they were overtaken by the elephants marching in single file towards their stables near Chelsea Old Church and stopping to drink at an Embankment fountain. 'Davies was enchanted with the cleverness of these animals,' wrote Osbert. He more than once referred to him as a man of genius. Towards the end of his autobiography Osbert summed Davies up: 'This extraordinary and memorable being, who, for all his humility, bore about him something of the primitive splendour and directness of the Elizabethan age . . . No one who knew him will, or ever could, forget him, even had he never written so many lovely poems.'[25] The Sitwells could be said to have been Davies's keenest fans, and largely through their kindness his London years after the war revolved around a remarkable circle of acquaintances.

Others saw him as an amusing eccentric, popular at parties for his apparent unworldliness and his Welsh story-telling ability. This fits too with the fact that he was much in demand to give public poetry readings. He enjoyed this; it brought him income, and through the readings he met other influential people (Ezra Pound was one who felt he had 'discovered' the Welshman through hearing him read). Often famous people would patronize him, and Davies would see through this but be happy to take advantage of their good nature. It was as important to him to be liked personally by the great and the famous as he felt it necessary for them to appreciate his poems.

There is a story of a famous actress at a dinner party giving an overblown rendition of 'Leisure', a poem crying out for understatement. In discussion afterwards a friend suggested that her reading had been insensitive. Davies was deeply offended and eagerly defended the performance.

From this period, too, dates a handwritten letter from him, one of the relatively few still in private hands. It appears to be a first manuscript of the poem 'How Kind Is Sleep' sent to the magazine *To-day*, signed 'Yours faithfully, William Davies', without the customary initial H. and amusing for its spelling error:

> So, every night deceived by sleep,
> Let me on roses lie;
> And leave the thorns of Truth for day,
> Too pierce me till I die.[26]

In 1921, when he turned fifty, Davies became briefly engaged to a Welsh girl; she is not named, and he says only that he thought better of proposing to her. It seems that he was seriously considering marriage and domestic comfort, but so far the right woman had not presented herself.

The year 1922 was another key year in his life. In it he moved to a better room in Brook Street, Mayfair; the long-established firm of Jonathan Cape took over the publishing of all his work; and a major American publisher, Yale University Press, brought out *The Captive Lion and Other Poems*, a selection of fifty poems from earlier collections, although omitting 'Leisure'.

In 1925 he published *Later Days*, his last major prose work, a slim volume of essays revisiting some of his tramping experiences, with a few descriptions of his forays into London high society. In an introduction he said that others had suggested he should write a book about his life since writing *The Autobiography of a Super-Tramp*. After some consideration (his words) he decided he could write it without 'trying to make common ditchwater sing like a pure spring'. What makes *Later Days* interesting eighty years on are the vignettes of famous writers whom he met socially in London throughout the postwar period and early 1920s.

One of the writers who frequented the Mont Blanc restaurant regularly before the war and who greatly impressed Davies was W.H. Hudson, whose *Green Mansions* Davies discovered only after he had known Hudson for about a year. He was indignant that no one had told him of the book; but the comment shows a typical lack of curiosity about the work of other writers. His excuse was that he could not afford to buy books and in any case 'I go to Life and Nature for my own ideas, and have no need of books.' This rather pompous pronouncement overlooks the fact that public libraries were in their heyday or that generous acquaintances regularly gave him books. He tells an anecdote about Hudson that illustrates Davies's peculiar sense of humour. Hudson half admiringly spoke of a peer's relative who had tried to balance a beer bottle on his nose at the Mont Blanc. Davies, somewhat bemused by titles and the aristocracy, reacted by suggesting indignantly that it was a perfectly natural thing for a peer's relative to do.

Another favourite haunt of Davies's was the vegetarian St George's Restaurant in St Martin's Lane, where Edward Thomas had once held court at tea parties. A particular friend here was Ralph Hodgson, the animal-loving poet, who would bring along his bull terrier Mooster – the Welshman was fond of them both, even to the extent of joining in late-night dog-walks. The two poets shared a passion for boxing and tobacco, Davies expanding at some length on the virtues of different brands.

On one occasion they argued about colour prejudice; Davies freely admitted to having retained some prejudice from his time in the USA and Hodgson put the opposing view. He accused Hodgson of having a reverse prejudice and of being unfair to whites. 'However, this was a dangerous subject, and we changed it almost immediately.'[27]

Indisputably Davies revelled in the company of famous authors. He had no hesitation in numbering himself as an equal among them, and yet he writes of them with genuine respect, fully aware of his indebtedness to men such as Edward Garnett, Edward Thomas and George Bernard Shaw. Shaw was to Davies a godlike figure, his mystery enhanced, so he claimed, by a nature as sympathetic as a woman's. He was in his element during these years, yet he still found it difficult to be at ease in London society with women, and often perceived slights where none were intended. To be befriended by such sympathetic society women as Edith Sitwell went a long way to lessen his unease with women, which was to have a consequence he could not have predicted.

Davies the Married Man

With this small house, this garden large,
This little gold, this lovely mate,
With health in body, peace at heart –
Show me a man more great.
                              – 'Truly Great'

DAVIES had two stabs at telling how he met and married his young wife when he was fifty-two, and both skate round the key facts. His earliest account was in *Later Days*, published only two years after his marriage. He was at the height of his literary output, with a dozen collections of poems to his name and a dozen editions of the *Autobiography*.

What he wrote in 1925 was 'I will now come to the greatest and happiest change in my life: a much greater and happier change than waking one morning . . . and finding myself the new and latest poet and the talk of London.' He goes on to say that he met Helen Payne, whom he thereafter calls Young Dinah, while he was ill. She came to visit him as often as she could, and they agreed to get married and live in a small country town. He decided she would make a good wife, he liked her disapproval of his drinking, and during his serious illness he was kept going by the prospect of marriage and life 'somewhere in the green country'. His most significant comment is 'How we met and where does not matter', and he reveals nothing of Helen's background except to say that she was a Sussex girl, so in Sussex they started married life 'leading a detached life in a semi-detached house'.[1]

In Sussex he recovered his health, and *Later Days* includes a pleasing portrait of marital domesticity, gardening, decorating the house for their first Christmas together and wrapping secret presents for one another. Indeed Davies demonstrates a childlike delight at the business of opening the presents on Christmas morning, watched by a dog named Beauty Boy and a black cat called Venus. He is revelling in the kind of childhood he never had as a boy, the chocolate animals, the sugar pigs, the paper chains and balloons. 'It was the most gorgeous room I had ever seen, and yet it was all built up with odd pennies.' The crowning excitement was pulling sixty-eight crackers, one of them two feet long.

It was an idyll summed up, as so often, in a short lyric:

> Here with my treasured Three I sit,
> Here in my little house of joy,
> Sharing one fire, and on one mat:
> My wife and my dog, Beauty Boy,
> And my black Venus of a cat.

The second verse reflects, unsophisticatedly, on which of the four will die first. It presents an idyllic picture of the marriage but an incomplete one.

A later and fuller version emerged three years later in the form of autobiography disguised as a novel, *Young Emma*, first offered to Jonathan Cape and then withdrawn. It was not to be published until 1980, forty years after Davies's death, and the story is a strange one.

In 1922 Davies was living in one room in Avery Row, Brook Street, Mayfair (he called it a mean little street yet within a stone's throw of 'one of the most fashionable quarters of the world'), and making occasional nightly forays into the Marble Arch area in search of female company. There is no doubt that in his fifties he was at last seriously considering marriage, but apart from the brief engagement to the Welsh girl, which ended amicably, he had not found himself a soulmate. Two women had refused him, and two he ruled out on the grounds that they were more interested in his celebrity than in him. One was an actress, but 'there could be no union between the footlights and a quiet study'. A slightly odd comment from one with the theatre in his blood.

Most of the women he met socially were already married or else they scared him. Prostitutes alarmed him less, and as far back as his American travels he had appreciated their company and even sought them out. Somewhere among those 'ladies of fashion' he felt he might find the right woman: 'I had made up my mind to find a woman to share my life . . . I made up my mind to trouble no more about respectable women, but to find a wife in the common streets.'[2]

This was during the war, when soldiers were a more attractive proposition than civilians. Add to this the fact that Davies was short, grey-haired, lame and shy, his chances of success with most women seemed slight. However, near Charing Cross Station he met and took a fancy to Bella, the wife of a sergeant-major who had just gone to the war, and they struck a deal whereby she would come to him twice a week, cook for him and collect whatever he could afford to give her. The arrangement ended when Davies discovered that she had stolen a parcel of linen, a clock and a bottle of whisky, replacing the contents with water. He viewed the affair philosophically, reflecting that it was much easier to get a mistress than a wife. 'Why was it so easy to get hold of other men's wives and not get one of my own?'[3]

His next lover was a Frenchwoman whom he called Louise. She stayed with him for a year, and he tells a touching story of her kissing the lips of his bronze Epstein bust when she was dusting. Her main defect was jealousy, and Davies well knew that she had another lover. After a year she left him for the other man, and for a time he missed her greatly, remembering her as the first woman who had shown him real affection. One or two other women of the street are mentioned in passing; Davies was apparently happy to invite them to his room, despite the fact that one was an alcoholic and another clearly deranged.

After these adventures he set out intentionally one night to find a young woman he could 'save' from the streets, as he put it.[4] Loitering at the Marble Arch end of the Edgware Road he watched a personable young woman get off a bus. She smiled at him, he raised his hat, she waited for him to overtake her, he asked her home. This then was the sudden and unlikely beginning of the romance between the poet and Helen Payne, which lasted for the rest of Davies's life. He admits that he was embarrassed to be seen late at night with a pretty girl half his age, but he felt sure that she was not a professional prostitute.

The question is, who exactly was Helen? There is the evidence of her death certificate that she was born on 4 August 1899 somewhere in Sussex. But searches of the official birth records for 1899 and 1900 reveal no child called Helen Matilda – the names recorded on their marriage certificate – whose birth was registered anywhere in England in those years. There are three Helenas and one Matilda but none born in Sussex. According to Davies, his wife came from the East Grinstead area, where three Paynes were registered in 1899; two were male babies and one was named Ellen Mabel. Is this coincidence, or did Davies change his wife's name on the wedding certificate? Helen was a name familiar to him from Helen Thomas, and Matilda was his sister's name; they are not totally dissimilar from Ellen Mabel. Nowhere again in any of his prose writing, or in the inscriptions in his books, does Davies refer to his wife as Helen: she is always Dinah, or later Emma. One cannot help speculating that they did not wish Helen's real name to be known. There is no evidence of any living relatives – and none attended their wedding – and she is not mentioned at all in Davies's *Who's Who* entry, written by him. When it came to signing the marriage register he could not remember her second name; perhaps Matilda came to mind spontaneously.

In his novel he gave her the fictitious name of Emma. Conceivably, this may have been her actual name, kept secret from their friends, or a disguised version of Ellen. When they first became acquainted 'Emma' told him she had a steady job in the city but lived with friends at the weekend; that she did not drink and had grown up on a farm in the country. Davies deduced that she was 'forced to occasional immorality' through poverty. The relationship developed, and 'Emma' became his housekeeper, giving him the pet name of 'Dear old Funny Cuts', later 'Bunnykins', while he called her 'Dinah'. Bunnykins and Dinah they were to remain.

If the novel is factually accurate, Davies developed venereal disease and septicaemia. He was seriously ill for some weeks, suffering also from depression, but Emma nursed him with care and devotion. Then it was her turn to be very ill, collapsing with acute pains one night. The woman who lived below Davies sent for a doctor who made a brief visit. Next morning the neighbour told Davies that his 'housekeeper' must get to hospital before she bled to death. She contacted several hospitals and even the police, but no bed was available. Davies, confined to bed himself, could do little to help. Finally a policeman on duty near by was persuaded to call and said he would send for a police ambulance if Davies would pay – adding that if she had been taken ill in the street she would have been taken to hospital for nothing. By the time she reached hospital it was seven hours after she had been taken ill, and even so the staff were reluctant to admit her. Only then did Davies, still helpless in bed, learn that Emma had had a miscarriage at six months. Evidently he had been unaware of her pregnancy. There is no reason to doubt his concern and surprise. He learned eventually that she had had a brief affair with an army officer who had promised to marry her when he was on leave but who had never returned. Davies seems to have accepted uncomplainingly her failure to tell him the whole story and shouldered without question responsibility for her welfare.

The novel provides insight into the inadequacy of medical services for poor Londoners in the years between the two world wars. There is no cause to doubt the verisimilitude of its account or to doubt that Helen would have died if Davies had not been able to pay for her to be admitted to hospital. As a result of her near death and his continuing illness they felt it would be best to move to the country, and Helen suggested her home county of Sussex.

Davies gave her the considerable sum of £15 to buy some basic household goods, which were transported to Sussex in a small motor van. Her lifelong devotion to him stemmed from his rescuing of her both from the streets and from certain death. As for him, he had at last found a woman for whom he could truly care. The age gap of twenty-eight years seemed unimportant. He described her as having 'a great heart and an affectionate spirit, and not a great brain . . . Our language was often nothing more than cuddles and kisses.'⁵

They settled into a semi-detached house in Cantelupe Road, East Grinstead, which delighted Helen because she now felt herself to be a real housewife, while it was the large garden that most pleased Davies. A dog and a cat completed the ménage. A garden became an absolute necessity in every home they had thereafter. The next step was to get married inconspicuously, so as not to draw the neighbours' attention to the fact that they had been living together unwed, and a late autumn wedding was planned. This plan was frustrated by Davies becoming ill again. He was too unwell to go far from home and consulted several doctors who offered various diagnoses. He mentions more than once that he feared madness and early death from venereal disease and considered separating from Helen to save her health. To this end he suggested to Helen that they should not make love for a while. Both of them had had active sexual pasts and had reason to be afraid of the consequences.

Helen was much distressed at Davies's apparent coolness, and when she set off for London to buy a coat he half expected her not to return. But she did come home, 'proud and happy, wearing her little ten-guinea fur coat'.[6] They celebrated Christmas together most contentedly, and soon after, on 5 February 1923, they were married at East Grinstead Register Office. Davies was fifty-two and Helen not yet twenty-four.

Their witnesses were Conrad Aiken, the American whose career as a poet Davies had helped to launch, and the writer Martin Armstrong who had been a friend for four or five years. Both of them happened to live in Sussex, fairly near East Grinstead, Aiken at Rye and Armstrong in Pulborough. Aiken at the time had just published *Modern American Poets*, and he was working on *Selected Poems of Emily Dickinson*. He went on to become one of the most distinguished American poets of his generation, winning a Pulitzer Prize and many academic awards. Martin Armstrong was a Cambridge-educated Newcastle man, at the time literary editor of the *Spectator*. He had served in the Artists' Rifles in France in 1915 and may have had contact with Edward Thomas there. Armstrong was mainly a poet, but he had published a life of George Borrow and in 1923 was compiling a selection of the works of Jeremy Taylor, the seventeenth-century divine and one-time chaplain to Charles I. A few years later he was to marry the first of Aiken's ex-wives, Jessie.[7]

Richard Stonesifer in his biography of Davies records that Aiken remembered the wedding day as a day of confusion, nervous embarrassment and misspelled names.[8] This may well have originated from the doubt about Helen's real name. They all went back to Torleven, Cantelupe Road, for port wine and cake, and the bridegroom gave the witnesses autographed copies of a second edition of *Foliage*, first published in 1913.

Shortly after this came new anxiety – the fear that Helen might previously have contracted a sexual illness from Davies. Her doctor dismissed the idea, prescribing medicine and advising long walks, which gave Helen the idea she would like a dog. One day she returned home with a very small puppy. In fact it transpired that Helen's illness was a minor one, and Davies's problem – septicaemia, contracted not from Helen but from a previous lover – eventually cleared up. Another of his ailments, rheumatism, however, continued to trouble him for the rest of his life.

The happiness of their married life continued for nearly twenty years, a way of life so different from Davies's earlier wandering days that he appeared to be a changed man. 'It seemed that I should be married to this child, who did not even have the courage to take a spoonful of medicine.' From the early anxious weeks Davies learned how meek and uncomplaining a wife he had found, one who could be made disproportionately happy by small gifts – a pair of shoes, a coat, a pet animal. Their love life was good, their relationship close and mutually devoted.

Davies ends *Young Emma* with the words: 'I have always been honest and sincere in my literary work, without thinking of popularity; and that, I suppose, is why I have remained poor.'

Some have wondered why the couple had no offspring. Davies gives no clue in any of his writings. That he was fond of children is implicit in his handing out of sweets to ones he met in Sevenoaks and in his attachment to Edward Thomas's young family. It may be that either he or Helen had been rendered infertile by their sexual illnesses, but there is no way of knowing whether this is the case.

In the next few years W.H. Davies, happily married man, published ten new works and several introductions to classics; he moved to a bigger home, Malpas House at Oxted in Surrey; and confirmed his status as a member of the London literary establishment.

A number of his poems refer to his happy domestic state and the joys of domesticity, as in 'Joy Supreme':

> The miser has his joy, with gold
> Beneath his pillow in the night;
> My head shall lie on soft warm hair
>
> . . .
>
> I shall lie near her, and feel
> Her soft warm bosom swell on mine.

Or the homely 'Knitting', where the poet watches his beloved 'stabbing the red wool and the white'. However much she nags, he still longs to be with her.

He was eagerly making up for the years of homelessness and lone-liness, and he shared with Helen a childlike pleasure in birthdays, Christmas, shopping and homemaking. She was no intellectual. It was said that each time he gave her a new book she cut the leaves but put it aside unread, and he quotes her asking ingenuously if he was as great as Shakespeare. But Davies did not look for intellectual companionship; he needed a loving companion to cook for him, mend his socks and share his bed. Helen was equally contented, according to those who knew them both. She had found love, security and a kind protector.

In fact this picture of quiet domestic happiness bears out the hope Davies had expressed in his bachelor days, in a letter to the critic Holbrook Jackson. He had envisaged a 'a little house with leafy eyes /That open to the southern skies', and ended the letter 'My dear Jackson, I wonder if you will like the enclosed ? With kind regards, W.H.D.'[9] Now and then in essays he gives a tolerant glimpse of Helen as ruling his life: she objected to his calling at pubs and to some of his old London friends, so that there could be no question of their returning to live in London. From Cantelupe Road in East Grinstead they had moved to Surrey and finally to Gloucestershire, a neutral territory for them both.

Meanwhile in 1922 Davies was asked to compile an anthology for the Poetry Bookshop, *Shorter Lyrics of the Twentieth Century*, in a limited edition of two hundred copies. In his foreword Davies wrote, 'As I am acting as critic in doing this anthology, my own contribution is one poem.'[10] This was 'The Kingfisher'. He added that he had been asked to include 'A Great Time', but he rejected this poem on the grounds that it had what he called 'a facile run' in the middle. False modesty? He stressed that this was an anthology of poetry, not poets, and listed his reject groups: patriotic verse (one he called 'a rhetorical jingle'), most war poems, free verse ('not poets at all') and anything purely descriptive.

Poems by Lascelles Abercrombie and Gordon Bottomley were omitted because of their length, and only a favoured few had four poems included: Robert Bridges, Walter de la Mare, Ralph Hodgson, John Masefield, W.B. Yeats and T. Sturge Moore. Others allowed three selections were Rupert Brooke, Alice Meynell, Ezra Pound, Edward

Thomas and Herbert Trench, plus a clutch of poets largely forgotten today or remembered for other reasons: Joseph Campbell, Michael Field, G. Hamilton Sorley and Alfred Douglas. It would seem the choices may, to some extent, have reflected Davies's personal friendships.

On the whole it was a reasonable cross-section of Davies's generation but with some unexpected omissions. There is nothing by W.H. Auden or T.S. Eliot, and Wilfred Owen is represented only by 'Anthem for Doomed Youth'. With one or two exceptions Davies kept to his brief. These poems are short, lyrical and written within the declared time-span. Aldous Huxley, James Joyce and Katherine Tynan might not come immediately to mind as lyricists, but their poems deserve inclusion. Two choices, however, strike the modern reader as extraordinary – Douglas Goldring's 'Merveilleuses de Nos Jours', in praise of early feminists, and M.M. Johnson's 'To a Fair Infant', sentimental verse addressed to a baby. Neither can be termed lyrics in the true sense of the word.

At about this time Davies wrote a eulogy of his late friend Edward Thomas, which he offered to Holbrook Jackson, then editor of the monthly magazine *To-day*. 'Thomas was too gentle and not blustering enough to compete with others who were less able to do the [journalistic] work. We find it the same when a big, saucy able-bodied beggar can make more money than even a man that is blind.'

He went on to analyse what made Thomas switch from prose to poetry. According to Davies, this was the influence of Robert Frost when Thomas and he became friends in Gloucestershire. 'Robert Frost was a great talker and a thoroughly good chap in every way. I may say here that Thomas was always influenced by good talkers, in spite of the few things they say that can be remembered. I have only met two, in my experience, that were really brilliant talkers; one was Edward Garnett, Thomas's friend and mine . . . and the other Walter Sickert.' Pursuing the topic of Frost's influence, Davies mentioned his surprise when he found Thomas working on a book of verse: 'I reminded him that the poets he had been slating for years were also reviewers . . . and they would all skin him alive.'

He recalled lunches on Tuesdays at London cafés with Thomas, Edward Garnett and W.H. Hudson and tea afterwards with Walter

Delamare [*sic*] and Ralph Hodgson. On one occasion they talked so long that the 'disgusted' waitresses piled up the chairs as a hint to them to leave. Referring to Thomas's sense of humour, Davies speculated on his character if he had not spent so much time with people of sharp wit. 'In his soldier's life he was meeting men of a plain simple humour, and I am certain he would have come out of the war, had he lived, a different man.'

The article ends with Davies's recollections of his last meeting with Thomas 'on the night when he was going to the Front. He had asked several friends to meet him, but for one reason or another only two came – Roger Ingpen and myself. I was suffering from great nervous fatigue on that occasion, for I had been sitting all day to Epstein for a portrait bust. But I was glad to be there, especially as his other friends had such important engagements. After Roger Ingpen had gone we walked up Charing Cross Road together, silent, and neither of us feeling comfortable. Probably I was the last of his old friends to wish him goodbye.'[11]

In 1923, a month or two after his marriage, Davies had offered his theatre project, *True Travellers: A Tramps' Opera*, to Clifford Bax, the author of *Polly*, and to Nigel Playfair, producer of a much-acclaimed version of *The Beggars' Opera*. They both told him it was unactable, but later that year Jonathan Cape published it in an attractive edition with illustrations by W.H. Nicholson. The most memorable of these is a sketch of a tramp of the 1920s, complete with battered boots, shapeless bowler hat, shawl over his ragged coat and possessions in an ancient Gladstone bag. The frontispiece is an impression of two tramps roused at dawn by the crowing of a vociferous cockerel.

Many would say that the drawings are the best part of the book. The three-act libretto amounts hardly to a plot – lodging-house keeper's daughter falls in love with educated penniless tramp, gypsy girl betrays the young man to the police, young man miraculously inherits money (from a South African uncle killed by falling over a nugget of gold) and becomes a benefactor to all his friends of the road. Most of the dialogue is in prose, interspersed with some forgettable jingles and one or two semi-philosophical monologues. Ralph's song to the gypsy Kate is one of the more pleasing ditties:

When autumn's fruit is packed and stored,
And barns are full of corn and grain;
When leaves come tumbling down to earth,
Shot down by wind or drops of rain:
Then up the road we'll whistling go,
And with a heart that's merry
We'll rob the squirrel of a nut,
Or chaffinch of a berry.

The three acts are a light-hearted cross between operetta and sociological study and interesting for the autobiographical touches that creep in. One act is set in a woodland beggars' camp, with 'several articles of clothes spread on the bushes around'. Beggars named Monkey Sam, the Professor and Snivelling Tom suggest characters Davies had met on the road. Snivelling Tom tells a tale of being given sixpence and a parcel of food to go away and stop singing: 'When I saw three sausages, four potatoes and six biscuits, I cried Halliujah [*sic*] . . . three times – although I am far from being a religious man.'

Two Sisters of Mercy and an organ grinder originate from his own experiences, and an occasional crude joke salts the dialogue. Old Martha the midwife tells the company in the lodging-house kitchen: 'My husband could hardly buy a new pair of trousers but what I had a baby . . . Roger, I said, don't buy two pairs unless you can afford to keep twins.'

There is a coarse reference to bishops and curates – 'a bishop usually has a redder nose and a larger belly than a curate' – and an anti-Semitic joke about Jews and pork. These remind the reader that Davies had led a rough life among rough travellers, a fact his often delicate lyrics tend to disguise.

The opera ends in a traditional, upbeat way with a cheerful duet between Dick and Dolly, the lovers, and Nicholson's fantasy views of insects – grasshoppers, dragonflies, butterflies – help to enhance the romantic element. The opera has curiosity value, but it is hardly surprising that it did not reach the stage.

Cape also brought out in 1924 *Secrets*, a small volume of new Davies poems, and soon after this Simpkin, Marshall published a collectors' edition of Defoe's *Moll Flanders*, with an introduction that begins in typical Davies style: 'We don't know whether Defoe had said to himself after he had written *Robinson Crusoe*, "I have written a book for boys and girls, and now I will write a book for women and men", for this he has certainly done; and there seems to be no more end to the popularity of one than to the other.' He makes it clear that he approves of Moll: 'In fact, if a man gave her a good home, with plenty to eat and drink, and was kind to her, she would never have divorced him for failing to do family duty . . . And seeing that she was well rewarded, and her body was no worse for what had been done to it, she had the satisfaction of having a new and exciting experience to relate to her friends.'[12] Given his sympathy for prostitutes, it is predictable to find Davies on Moll's side.

The year 1925 was one of achievement for Davies. In it he published *Later Days*, the memoir that in many ways complemented the *Autobiography*, as well as an introduction to a collection of Robert Burns poems and his own very personal *A Poet's Alphabet*. This was illustrated with pen and ink sketches by Dora Batty, who showed herself much in tune with Davies. Each letter of the alphabet inspired a brief verse entirely characteristic of the author.

> B is for Beauty – My girl has reached that lovely state / That's half a bud and half a flower / But I am near my berry time.
> F is for Fiddles – To hear a Master's hand express / That very soul and tenderness.

The letter R refers to his father Francis, still remembered with a child's affection fifty years after his death. 'R is for Remembrance – All I remember is a coat / Of velvet, buttoned on his breast, / Where I, when tired of fingering it / Would lay my childish head and rest.' (He goes on to recall his father's loud consumptive cough, making children think of monsters growling.)

Other verses are less autobiographical and certainly less conventional. I is for Implements, contrasting a spade shiny with use to a rusted sword. J is for Jealousy: the poet's spiteful lady mowed his daisies, bought a cat, cut down his flowers – yet still he loved her. Q is for Question: is there an after-life? he asks a ghost. And in W for Will,

Davies set out his wish to leave his beloved a small house and a little money, wishing he could also bequeath her his joy in nature.

Not all the critics praised his work. Katherine Mansfield found him 'something childish', and J.C. Squire rather cruelly parodied Davies:

> He does not eat
> In cosy inns,
> But keeps his meat in salmon tins.[13]

C. Henry Warren, in *The Bookman* of December 1925, had this to say of Davies: 'To read of him hobnobbing with literary giants like Conrad and Hudson, Ralph Hodgson and de la Mare, is almost to conjure up the picture of a bright-eyed bird threading dexterously through the traffic of Piccadilly.'[14]

Davies defended himself in print from time to time, most cogently in a *New Statesman* article towards the end of 1923, in which he argues that it may take generations for a writer's true greatness to be recognized ('even now we are not sure that Shakespeare is given credit for all his qualities').[15]

In *Later Days* he lists the questions that might be put to him beyond the grave: how did he deceive the public for so long? How did he persuade so many great artists to paint his portrait? How did he acquire a Civil List pension? His answer would be to recite some of his best poems, and he was well aware that he had written many inferior ones. He approved of the critic who said he stood for 'human nature simple and unspoiled'.

A Poet's Alphabet was followed two years later by *A Poet's Calendar*, again with illustrations by Dora Batty. The format is rather similar, with two postage-stamp-sized sketches and two poems standing for each month. Some of the thoughts and images are conventional, but many verge on the bizarre. February refers to bird-scaring; a small girl may clap her hands to shoo the birds away, but if she does this in old age she is perceived as crazy. In March the story told is of two men, one living on a hill, one in a valley, who daily changed places to view their homes from a different perspective. The June poem is 'Property' – the illustration shows a squirrel with nuts (a favourite image with Davies), and the verse has these perhaps resentful lines:

> A poet with five houses, Lord
>
> . . .
>
> Should at the least expect in rent
>
> A shilling for his dinner . . .

but the hens (the five providers) lay eggs for his trustee, not for the poet.[16] There is more than a hint here of that bitterness which Davies felt towards others who found money came to them more easily than it did to him.

September calls up the music of the spheres, the evening star, birds and moon. Unexpectedly the illustration is of a banjo. November deals with fire:

> I'll turn that black-faced nigger, Coal
>
> Into an Indian painted red
>
> And let him dance and fire wildshots
>
> Into the chimney overhead'

The illustration shows a Native American warrior-archer, reminiscent of Hiawatha.

Yet for all its fantasy and wit, *A Poet's Calendar* ends on a sombre note: 'On Christmas Day I sit and think / Thoughts White as Snow, and Black as Ink.'[17]

The contrasts in the *Calendar* as a whole echo Davies's periods of happiness and depression. Night is equated with blindness, a white horse portends death, a decorated tombstone reminds the poet that 'one by one my friends leave home'.

The collection was published in 1927, but the morbid verses may have been written earlier, before Davies settled down and became domesticated. Morbidity is a strong element in many of his seven hundred poems, though nowhere as strongly felt as in 'The Lodging House Fire'.

> My mind durst know no thought –
>
> It knew my life too well;
>
> 'Twas hell before, behind,
>
> And round me hell.

In 1927 Davies's second novel was published. An astute reader would have no difficulty in recognizing that *Dancing Mad* was by the same author as *A Weak Woman*, and it recapitulates much of Davies's own history. This, again, is an unsubtle story with splashes of melodrama. The preamble announces:

> *Dancing Mad*, the story of trouble between a man and his high-minded wife ... is told with a direct intensity that makes the feelings of ordinary characters seem anaemic beside those of Norman and Nancy. Mr Davies's heroine dances away her home ... and later is forced to dance to another tune. Her husband is not a man for half measures.

The novel tells the story of Norman Beresford, an artist, and his girl friend Mildred. It is Mildred who is 'dancing mad' and who drives Norman from home with her obsession. He burns his paintings and flees to Mississippi, living as a hobo. Here the autobiographical references are quite explicit: camping in the woods, drifting down the river, contracting malaria, railriding, returning to London to take up writing.

In the seven years of Norman's absence Mildred has met an old admirer with whom she dances at the Café Royal before marrying him. Later, feeling remorse, she searches for Norman; he has a job as a ship's cattleman on a boat called the *Minniesota* [*sic*] and earns money as a pavement artist.

Eventually they meet again; Norman rejects her; the bigamous Mildred descends into madness and begs both her husbands for forgiveness – dying at the moment of possible reconciliation. Norman joins the army and is killed in France – later it transpires that two admirers of his work as a pavement artist believe him to have been a neglected genius.

Two contemporary comments give cause for surprise. One critic wrote 'What a lesson Mr Davies here reads to modern couples!' and another 'He has it in him to write a far more powerful novel than people wot of.' In fact the book has little merit except as a fictional reworking of parts of *The Autobiography of a Super-Tramp*. Davies had a feel for narrative drama but not the instinct to avoid melodrama.

The Adventures of Johnny Walker, Tramp, published in 1926, has particular relevance to Davies's efforts at writing fiction. The introduction is a kind of disclaimer for *A Weak Woman*:

A few people, perhaps a very few, will remember that my *Autobiography of a Super-Tramp* was followed by three other books of prose, two of them dealing with my own tramping experiences, and the other being a novel. We will say no more about the novel, and regard it as a pest to be exterminated at sight. I will go so far as to offer twopence for every front page that comes my way, in the same way as we offer a penny for the tail of every rat that is killed. If any of my readers are fortunate enough to get possession of a score or more of that particular novel, and send the front pages to my publisher for a reward, they will be doing more good to the community than any ratcatcher that ever lived, although he boasts of 20,000 tails.[18]

Hyperbole? Mock modesty? A perverse attempt to gain publicity? Whatever the motive, it did not deter readers from buying *The Adventures of Johnny Walker, Tramp*, described by Davies as somewhere between essay form and story form. In fact it is a follow-up to *Beggars*, drawing on some material from there and some from *The Autobiography of a Super-Tramp*. In his foreword he defends the format by saying he has pulled the previous writings together in story form: 'For the younger generation it will of course be a new book, and should come between the *Autobiography* and *Later Days.*'

A few new sidelights are thrown on Davies's American travels: the time when he was paid £2 for a trip as night watchman on a Mississippi cattle boat; the financial benefits of fruit-picking in Texas; his encounters with Oklahoma Sam and Red-nosed Scotty. One story appears to be new in this book – the tale of Irish Paddy and Bridget Mahoney, characters met in a Chicago soup kitchen. She says of her man that if he had paid as much attention to the Bible as he did to her legs when they were courting 'he'd be Pope of Rome now'.

Chicago was also where Davies had met Sullivan. This was the plausible beggar who took to haunting a certain mission hall where good soup was served, where he astonished his mates by making a public confession of his sins and appearing on the platform in smart clothes. Subsequently he was to open the meetings in prayer and lead the hymns; finally he announced his engagement to the wealthy widow who financed the mission. One wishes that Davies had written more about this opportunistic character.

He notes that American prisons are apt to be thought of as 'hotels for comfort', and he was in the habit of regarding prisons as free bed and breakfast accommodation. Not in the so-called coolers of the Southern states. In one such he and Brum were shocked to be locked in an unlit cell on a freezing night with two-and-a-half evil-smelling blankets between them: 'this was downright cruelty'.

One of his most vivid pictures in *The Adventures of Johnny Walker, Tramp* is of the Old Prison in New Orleans, normally reserved for blacks and poor whites. Davies was gaoled there for thirty days after being caught sleeping in a freight car. The judge ('an old Southerner who could never forgive the North for freeing the slaves without giving their owners some compensation') resented beggars coming from the North to milk the Southern states. In this gaol Davies was fed only bread and greasy water, a near-starvation diet, in weather so cold the offenders could not sleep at night. He tells the pathetic story of a crazy Chinese prisoner who could speak no English and communicated with no one except at intervals to 'sing his grief like a bird'. After a night of snow the prisoner was found dead, in his cell, yet snow-covered. Davies reckoned this was the most pathetic man he had ever seen, no light statement.[19] Another grim tale is Davies's account of riding the rods in Texas.

Most of the book consists of recycled stories, and anyone who has read *The Autobiography of a Super Tramp* will not find much entirely new material. Indeed most of Davies's publications from 1922 onwards consist of reissues or reworked old stories.

In 1928 he was nearing sixty, and at Helen's insistence he was thinking of moving away from the south-east of England. Partly she was motivated by unease when she met his literary friends, partly by a wish to live more stylishly as the wife of a famous author and to shake off her past altogether. Whatever the incentive, it was Helen who initiated this final move. And so just after Davies's fifty-seventh birthday they went westwards to find their ideal home.

Nailsworth in the 1930s

Today I have played truant from my garden, and gone two or three
miles away to see the river Severn lying in a green valley, and still a long
way off ... The sight of this river, the Severn, as seen from a hill in Monmouthshire, in my young days, is still fresh in my memory, and not
likely to be forgotten. And that is why I make this pilgrimage today, and
will do it again, and still again.

– My Garden

THE Davies who went house-hunting in Nailsworth in the Stroud valleys in the autumn of 1928 was seemingly a very different character
from the down-and-out who had trudged from door to door around
the Midlands and the Thames Valley begging in the early years of the
century. He was now an established writer with a steady income, an
attractive wife and appearances to keep up among his friends and
acquaintances, some of whom were household names.

He was advised on finding a home by J.W. (John) Haines, a
Gloucester lawyer and amateur botanist, friend of poets and a poet
himself, who did much to help the Dymock group and to support the
Gloucestershire poets Ivor Gurney and F.W. Harvey; in fact Harvey
worked as a solicitor for Haines. (It was with Haines that Edward
Thomas had spent three days walking in the Forest of Dean in June
1915, before writing his famous poem 'Words' and making up his
mind to join the army.)

Haines said later that Davies asked his advice on choosing a home
'near to Wales but not in Wales'.[1] In middle age (he was now fifty-
seven and fast turning grey) he felt less empathy with the Welsh and
did not want to be haunted by ghosts from his past. Haines, with all
his literary friends, was an ideal contact for Davies in his new community, a wise friend as well as a good lawyer.

Davies would have been interested in two items appearing in *The
Times* around the time of his move. One was an article drawing attention to the acute distress in the South Wales valleys following the
wholesale closure of mines and shops, citing a figure of 80,000 unemployed out of a population of 200,000. The other was a column-long

review of a book of memoirs by the poet Edmund Blunden, *Undertones of War*, recalling the lives of ordinary soldiers in the trenches.

Nailsworth was by now reduced to a quiet market town of grey Cotswold cottages and Victorian and Edwardian villas, with a population approaching 3,000. The wool industry had declined, and modern technology had not yet turned the area into the centre of light industry it was to become after the Second World War. During Davies's lifetime it acquired a new Baptist chapel (the old one, the Tabernacle, was first taken over by the Wesleyans and then took on a new lease of life as the Town Hall), a Victorian vicarage, a modernized police station and a Court House. The town was big enough for Davies and Helen not to feel conspicuous as newcomers, small enough for them to feel immediately at home.

Some of the bigger mills were still active when the couple arrived but now making mainly shoddy – an inferior form of plush – or walking-sticks and umbrellas. Others had been converted into hotels, rural workshops or private houses. The bacon factory (locally known as 'The Trade') had increased in size to provide many more jobs than it had done sixty years earlier. Meanwhile the brewery flourished, and another local product was leatherboard, a kind of imitation leather. Nailsworth no longer clattered and sent up plumes of smoke from so many factories, but it had full employment and a clutch of relatively new shops.

There was a draper and milliner to cater for Helen's love of clothes-buying and a tobacconist to supply her husband, as well as a stationer who kept him in brown-covered exercise books in which he meticulously copied out his poems in a small neat hand and gave them to his wife, with inscriptions such as 'To Dinah from Bunny' or 'From Bunnykins to his Dinah'.[2] The origin of these pet names seems to be derived from an American folk song, 'Billykins and His Dinah', and Davies never seems to have addressed his wife in any other way, at least on paper. The exercise books, later handed on to Helen's heir, are the closest things to love letters that survive, and they make clear the couple's abiding affection for each other.

Nailsworth also had a pharmacy owned by a Chipping Campden man, Louis E. Wixey. The oldest of his four daughters, Marjorie, helped in the shop and sometimes delivered prescriptions to special

clients. Elderly residents remember Mr Wixey as a courteous gentleman, much concerned for his customers. Many of them regarded the
pharmacist as a substitute for the local doctor. His youngest daughter,
Peggy (now Peggy Drake), described a meeting she had with the poet
in September 1939. 'I was visiting my family from Birmingham, and I
wanted to ask for his autograph in my copy of his *Collected Poems*. My
sisters told me I wouldn't get anywhere near him. They said that Mrs
Davies was a bit of a dragon and kept everyone away, so I went along
in some trepidation. His house was just round the corner from our
shop. To my surprise he opened the door at Yewdales himself – a very
ordinary-looking little man. He didn't ask me in, but he asked me
quite kindly to leave the book with him. I think one of my sisters collected it, and he'd written "Good luck from W.H. Davies, 20th March,
1939."'[3]

The Wixey family lived at Jubilee Cottage on Tabrams Pitch until
their father's death in 1950. Mrs Drake recalled clearly the pharmacy
in Bridge Street: 'Coming from Stroud there was a builder's yard, then
a tailor, a baker-confectioner, our shop and on the corner a gents' out-
fitter called Dauncey. Mr Dauncey had a house on Watledge [where
the Davieses later lived], and I believe he knew the Davieses well.'
Bridge Street has been much altered and is now being refurbished,
none of the shops Mrs Drake recalls having survived. As well as the
premises she mentions, an ironmonger, a newsagent and a furniture
shop were also near by. The Davieses did not have to walk far for their
everyday needs.

One can picture them arriving by train, for Nailsworth in 1928 had
a station and its own five-mile branch line from Stonehouse, linking
up with the London–Bristol Great Western main line. There were two
intermediate stops, at Dudbridge in Stroud and the village of Woodchester, notable for its important Roman mosaic pavement in its
churchyard. Between the wars the pavement was uncovered to the
public once every ten years, and Davies probably saw it. A two-coach
train known as the Dudbridge Donkey provided a well-used shuttle
service between Stonehouse and Nailsworth, once a decade bringing
the sightseers to Woodchester. The line closed only a few years after
Davies died; the goods yard is now a restaurant car park, and
Nailsworth Fire Station stands on part of the approach road. Some

buildings remain more or less unchanged: a coal depot ('L. Jones, builder and coal merchant – truck loads at colliery prices') and the one-time Railway Hotel, rather forlorn now but with tall black lettering painted on the walls proclaiming its former identity. The station itself is now a private house, retaining the Gothic porch of the old stationmaster's house, a pillared main entrance and traces of platform and the bed of the rail track.

In 1928 most people travelled by rail; certainly Davies and his wife did. From the handsome Victorian station they might have called in at the Railway Hotel for refreshments before taking a taxi to Shenstone, later called Axpills House, a Victorian villa just off Cossack Square. The Davieses rented part of Axpills House, looking across to the early eighteenth-century Britannia Inn and the Jacobean Wool Loft and close to the seventeenth-century Friends' Meeting House. This was one of the earliest permitted Quaker meeting places in the country; these days it is a tourist attraction as well as being the focus of an active group of Friends.

The Davieses did not socialize much locally; but they kept in close touch with their Gloucester solicitor and friend John Haines, with other writers based in Gloucestershire and a few London friends. A particular crony was Brian Waters, a writer living outside Gloucester at a farm on Dundry Hill near the Welsh border. A decade after Davies's death he was to publish a selection of the poet's best work, with an adulatory introduction referring to him curiously as 'about the last of England's professional poets'.[4] Waters also provided a portrait of the poet in his old age:

> His skin was on the dark side and had the ruddy glow of full blooded health. His forehead was finely shaped and surmounted by a crest of iron grey hair. Character and personality rather than good looks were the keynote to his expressive face. No one . . . could have mistaken him for other than a Newport man, for apart from intonation he pronounced such words as man and Japan with the exaggerated long *a* of Gwent.[5]

The writer alleged that the poet's grandmother had once described the boy prophetically as a 'rodney' (a Newport word for a tramp).

Waters viewed the years that the author spent as a hobo in America as wasted, not recognizing how much rich material they yielded for his writing later on in life. He played down 'the story of the poet-tramp' and his prose 'classics of English and American vagrancy' as providing a misleading view of Davies's talent. He saw Davies as a born writer, and his sometimes extravagant praise must be read with caution.

When Davies stayed at Waters's home he could see the distant Newport transporter bridge across the Severn, very close to his birthplace. This did not arouse nostalgia; according to Waters, the poet 'preferred the intimate in scenery'. Among other reminiscences Waters mentioned Davies's known abhorrence for the telephone (mentioned also by Osbert Sitwell). He refused to use it even though there was one in the house. Waters interpreted his frequent housemoving as a sign of his restless nature, not of discontent. One anecdote describes the poet out walking to visit a neighbour and 'looking very dapper in a new grey suit that toned with the plumage of his hair', observing with satisfaction that a conceited man they passed had now discovered that 'he was not the best-dressed man in Nailsworth'.

In 1929 Davies wrote introductions to reissues of two classics which were felt to be relevant to him: Daniel Defoe's novel *Moll Flanders,* first published in 1750, and *A Greene Forest, or a Naturall Historie,* by John Maplet, reprinted in facsimile from a 1567 edition. The Maplet book had notes on many natural phenomena in alphabetical order. Davies's views on sexual fantasy make interesting reading. Of the female rogue Moll Flanders he wrote that ('to my own knowledge') some men found their sexual excitement in slapping and making prostitutes scream, 'but if this man had met Moll Flanders what would have been the result? For although Moll, if given the hint, would have screamed lustily for good money, I very much doubt whether she would have done so from fear.'[6] He much admired the illustrations in the 1929 edition, which to him showed a 'woman of the world with a sane mind, and full of power . . . as remote from the giddy flirt as she is from the innocent virgin'.

After a year or two at Axpills (then called Shenstone) Davies and Helen moved to leafy Spring Hill, to another solid and comfortable rented Victorian villa, and then briefly to The Croft. As none of these homes was far apart it seems likely they moved on when the leases expired. Their fourth home in Nailsworth was Yewdale (now called The Yewdales), with a Tudor façade facing Market Street. Photographs show the poet smoking his pipe in a relaxed manner under the Tudor arch. It was when he went shopping or stood in his doorway smoking that Davies became something of a familiar figure to Nailsworth residents, unobtrusive but very recognizable. He made few public appearances but now and then visited the local school to read his poems to the children, as older residents recall. He was also seen sometimes at the George pub, quietly enjoying a pint and a smoke, or out walking with his dog.

Finally, in 1939, the couple bought Glendower on Watledge from Raphael Ushaw Harrison, a marine engineer who had lived there for twenty years. Glendower had an interesting history, being built well before 1800, perhaps in the mid seventeenth century, probably as a weaver's cottage. By 1879 it was tenanted jointly by four tradesmen: Thomas Ford, described as a cloth factor, Samuel Reynolds, a fly-driver, Ebenezer Chandler, a carpenter, and Joseph Clift, an innholder. Twenty years later Glendower was inherited by a widow, Eliza Dean, who improved the cottage with money borrowed from a Stroud pork butcher.[7] At about this time half of Glendower became a shop or general store, and the bow window and front door of the shop can still be seen. In 1919 Raphael Harrison paid £376 for 'a shop and premises'. He had a mortgage of £240, and it seems that he did not continue to run the shop. This property, with its substantial though steeply sloping garden, was acquired by the Davieses for £450. It was their ideal home: a double-fronted greystone cottage perched on a quiet lane running along the side of the valley (the 'little house with leafy eyes' he had dreamed of in a letter ten years earlier to Holbrook Jackson). It stood well above the Bath Road, with stunning views close by and its pleasant but very steep garden divided into terraces.

A former neighbour, Eileen Ponting, remembered him walking past her home on his way to the Shearers Inn (long since vanished), also on Watledge. He would chat with her eleven-year-old brother about his American travels – 'he used to say he travelled all over the States without ever paying. They said at the Shearers he never needed to buy a drink. And when he left the pub it was his habit to walk up a nearby hill to sit and stare at the view. As I recall, he had a weather-beaten complexion and bushy hair; he was quite a short man.'

It has been suggested that Davies settled into a life of 'industrious leisure', writing only when the mood seized him. Yet he was a prolific poet, and a good deal of his verse work was composed in the last ten years of his life. Brian Waters, who knew him well during this period, describes his rapid creativity ('his prose writings were for him inter-ludes, brisk and swift departures from his life as a poet') and the fact that when he found himself unable to spell a word he simply resorted to a simpler one. When he stayed with Waters at Dundry Hill he could look across the Severn towards Newport, but he regarded his native place as 'far away and long ago'.

It was important to Davies to be known as a poet and to associate with other poets of repute. On one occasion he visited Clevedon in Somerset, where he found the people uninspiring until it was pointed out to him that Coleridge had lived there. This delighted him, as he regarded 'The Rime of the Ancient Mariner' and 'Kubla Khan' as two of the finest poems written in English. Waters commented: 'He was among the least humble of men.'[8] He must have been mortified by Robert Graves's dismissive reference in his *Survey of Modernist Poetry* to the 'simple ruralities of W.H. Davies' and objected strongly to being classified by others as merely a nature poet.[9]

Barely a year after settling in Nailsworth Davies was awarded an honorary doctorate of literature at the University of Wales. He went to Cardiff on 20 July 1929 for the ceremony at the City Hall, where the citation described him as 'a poet of distinction and a man in whose work much of the peculiarly Welsh attitude to life is expressed with singular grace and sincerity'. He was presented to the Vice-Chancellor as having rediscovered 'the joys of simple nature for those who had forgotten them . . . and in an age that is mercenary reminds us that we have the capacity for spiritual enjoyment'. The speaker concluded: 'I present him to you, that the University of a people that loves beauty and homeliness may do honour to one that has inter-preted its spirit to the wider world, and has revealed it to itself.' Although he now could call himself Dr Davies, he chose not to do so.

A photograph published in the *Western Mail and South Wales News* at the time shows a self-possessed small man in cap and gown, grasping a walking stick and a scroll, surrounded by dignitaries much taller than himself. One of the other six recipients of honorary degrees was the Lord Chancellor, Lord Sankey, and the headline ran 'Nation's Tribute: Honour to Whom Honour Is Due'.[10] The ceremony ended with a college choir singing 'Tri Bar Gwyr Morganwy'. What particularly pleased Davies was that his honorary degree came from the university of the capital of Wales and that it had been a thoroughly Welsh occasion.

As his fame grew locally, so his autograph was increasingly in demand, and amateur writers sent their work to him for approval. A typical reply was sent from Shenstone on 15 October, 1930, to a Mr J. Ashleigh: 'Dear Mr Ashleigh, Of course I remember you, and also our conversation. I am almost afraid to read your "Rambling Kid", for fear it breaks up my home by starting me on the road again. However I will tackle it as soon as I can, when I have finished a little awkward job that I have in hand. Yours sincerely, W.H. Davies.'[11]

At this time also Davies was reaching a wider public through successive editions of his poems and through broadcasts made for BBC Radio Wales. His first radio reading of his poems, transmitted from London in 1924, included fifteen poems, among them 'The Kingfisher' and 'Days That Have Been'. This was followed a year later by a discussion on verse-reading with the actor Miles Malleson and Harold Monro of the Poetry Bookshop. In December 1933 he broadcast another batch of poems, travelling to London to record them, and in 1937 he undertook his first broadcast for BBC Wales: twenty poems, including 'Days That Have Been', 'Sheep', 'The Kingfisher', 'Leisure' and 'The Moon'. Welsh listeners demanded a repeat, and more poems were broadcast in February 1938.

Later that year Davies recorded a talk for BBC Midland. It was announced as 'Time Turns Back: The Trial of William Shakespeare for Deer-Stealing', and it was broadcast nationally early in 1939. He was in fact repeating a favourite Shakespeare myth for which there is only circumstantial evidence. In October and November 1938 he recorded a series of readings from *The Autobiography of a Super-Tramp*, and two months later he read a selection entitled 'Love Poems by Dead Masters'. In 1939 he shared a recording studio with John Moore, the Tewkesbury poet and novelist and biographer of Edward Thomas.

Apart from repeats Davies's last recording, a reading of five poems ending with 'Dreamers', went out in October 1940, a week after his death and during the Battle of Britain.[12]

The recordings have stood the test of time well: the slow rhythm of his voice, strong even in his sixties but by then slightly husky, have an appealing quality, and from time to time his readings are broadcast today.

His home life was more comfortable than it had ever been. He pottered in the garden, walked about the town and relied on Helen to keep him well fed and content. For a time they could afford the luxury of two maids, something undreamed of in the early years of their marriage; a typical annual wage for a cook was £52. Their housekeeper, Florence Shilham, of Rodmarton, in a radio interview years later recalled what life was like with them. 'I was a cook-general. I did the housework, the fires, cooking, and waiting at table. We had a morning uniform and an afternoon uniform. Everything had to be just right. They liked straightforward food, especially potato and onion pie.' She mentioned the occasional visitors who came, but the couple were entertained more often than they played hosts to others.

Some insight into Davies's domesticated life in this decade can be gleaned from two small books published in 1933, *My Garden* and *My Birds*. Six years later they were combined in one volume with charming woodcuts of birds by Hilda M. Quick. Davies was always fortunate in his illustrators. The two collections amount to no more than unsophisticated nature notes, such as might have appeared in a local paper. They are observations of wildlife observed in his Nailsworth gardens, and Davies admits in an introduction that he was no scientist. 'It is sufficient for me to know that rabbits don't lay eggs.' Apart from a section on parrots (recalling his grandfather and the sailors he knew as a boy in Newport) all the anecdotes refer to common garden birds – blackbirds, robins, sparrows, owls, magpies – with a short article on the habits of cuckoos. Birds are observed courting, feeding and even dead. Some of the blame for their demise is attached to Davies's pets, Betty, a sealyham, and Pharaoh, a black cat. Pets figured largely in Davies's homes and his writings, although he knew he might be accused of sentimentality. Invariably the ménage included a dog and a black cat. One anecdote has the author marvelling at Pharaoh's eagerness to chase after another animal's food when his own diet is entirely composed of liver and fish.

There is a touch of absurdity in the short verse with which Davies begins *My Birds*, where he tells the story of a poet calling at his house dressed for some official function, only to have his top hat spattered with bird droppings. The book ends with a gruesome account of a man who stole and boiled cats for food.

My Garden is even shorter, concerned again with birds but also with flowers, foxes and a gypsy couple selling firewood who called at his house. The author mentions being pleased with himself for spotting that the man claimed to have five children to support while his wife in her sob-story alluded to just three. The book ends with a macabre account of fighting breaking out at an Irish wake that he attended as a very small boy. Elsewhere he gives advice on maintaining a garden and reminisces on his pleasure in making a garden seat. He advocates minimal weeding. This, he insists, is only necessary where weed-killer cannot be sprinkled. These two books do little for Davies's reputation, yet they have a certain naive appeal.

From time to time the couple visited Davies's nephew and family at Stonehouse, seven miles away at the other end of the branch railway. Noel Phillips, an engineer, was the son of Davies's sister Matilda, who had married Trevor Phillips and had four children. Noel, the oldest, was born in 1896, and he married Margery Adkins, born in 1899. They had two sons, John and Norman, born in 1932 and 1934, and lived near Stonehouse Station in the 1930s. Photographs show the poet and Helen playing with two small boys in a garden with stone garden ornaments. One of the small boys, Norman, was given a toy tractor by his great-uncle for his sixth birthday. These days Norman Phillips is the sole owner of Glendower, where he has lived for fifty years, although he has relatively few of his great-uncle's possessions. There is the half-grandfather clock given to Davies by the people of Newport, a jug-shaped umbrella stand and a plain sideboard. Everything else Helen sold off or took with her when she left the house. Some years later Glendower was bought by Norman's mother to keep it in the family.

More frequently the Davieses visited Nether Lypiatt Manor, a handsome William-and-Mary mansion high on the Cotswolds across the valley from Stroud. This was the home of Violet Gordon Wood-house, famous in her day as a talented harpsichordist, a salon hostess and a woman who shared her home virtually all her married life with a husband and two other men (there had been three until one was killed in the First World War). Gordon Woodhouse managed the house and brought great knowledge of décor, food and wine to the household; Bill, Viscount Barrington, designed the garden and ran the home farm; while Dennis Tollemache organized Violet's concerts and recitals. Davies came to know them all well – he had first met them at one of Violet's London salons – and one can imagine what satisfaction it gave him to attend dinner parties in this elegant setting, the house opulently furnished by Violet, the walled garden beautifully laid out by Bill.[13]

In 1933 Nether Lypiatt was visited by his old friends Osbert and Edith Sitwell who had been staying at Badminton, home of the Duke of Beaufort, at the same time as Queen Mary. Violet, who had only recently discovered the poet to be a virtual neighbour, invited the Davieses over for a reunion. Accepting the invitation, the poet, disingenuous as ever, wrote: 'Fancy two celebrities of our note living so close and not knowing it!'

It was through Violet that he had formed his lifelong attachment to all three Sitwells whom he had first met at the home of Osbert and Sacheverell in Carlyle Square, Chelsea, around 1915. It was there that he first encountered Violet, and she had encouraged his friendship with the Sitwell family. To Davies Edith was always 'as fine as a queen'. Osbert later in life listed Davies among his eminent dinner party guests.

Edith gave tea parties – or salons – in Pembridge Mansions, Bayswater, and there Davies met some of the artists who later painted him. In innumerable ways the Sitwell family helped to promote Davies as a poet, to act as his mentors and to introduce him to artistic society.

In 1921, not long before Edith gave her first memorable perfor-mance of *Façade*, she had been visited in London by a young cousin by marriage, Constance Sitwell. The latter wrote in her diary: 'I went to tea with Edith . . . Edith read "The Kingfisher" of W.H. Davies beautifully. It really was lovely.' Also in that year Edith wrote to a new young protégé, Brian Howard: 'Will you come with me to a meeting of the Anglo-French Poetry Society and hear William Davies read his poems, Mrs Arnold Bennett recite, and meet them both?'[14]

So Davies and Edith were overjoyed to meet again in 1933 at Nether Lypiatt Manor, where, according to her, 'An old and reverenced friend came over to see us, William Davies the poet. We sat talking till two in the morning, and I am afraid our hostess was worn out.' In the same letter to Allen Tanner, an American pianist, she described Davies as one of the four finest living English poets.[15] She does not indicate who the others were in her estimation. Certainly he featured strongly in Edith's *Aspects of Modern Poetry* of 1934, and although the book had had a mixed reception among critics and fellow-poets it did Davies's reputation no harm. Osbert recorded that on his first visit to Nether Lypiatt Violet showed Davies a small ship in a bottle. His response was: 'Do you come of seafaring folk, too?'

Probably the most important literary influence the Nether Lypiatt household had on Davies was to inspire his poem 'On Hearing Mrs Woodhouse Play the Harpsichord'. This is notable for breaking away from his usual subject-matter. The second verse is rather trite ('My music / . . . Has made this poet my dumb slave'), but the first verse reminds one a little of the Metaphysical Poets of the seventeenth century:

> We poets pride ourselves on what
> We feel, and not what we achieve;
> The world may call our children fools,
> Enough for us that we conceive.
> A little wren that loves the grass
> Can be as proud as any lark
> That tumbles in the cloudless sky,
> Up near the sun, till he becomes
> The apple of that shining eye.

Other contemporary writers who lived or stayed in the south Cotswolds during the Davieses' time at Nailsworth included Max Beerbohm and John Masefield . The Masefields rented Pinbury Park, near Cirencester, on the Bathurst estate, from 1933 to 1939. It was a large seventeenth-century house previously inhabited by leading members of the Arts ands Crafts Movement and said to be haunted by nuns – it had once been a nunnery. It is inconceivable that Davies did not visit there, since the Masefields' tenancy coincided exactly with his own time in Nailsworth. Then there were William Rothenstein and Max Beerbohm at Far Oakridge, only a few miles away. It was here that Davies had had his portrait painted by Rothenstein on earlier visits to Iles Farm, a seventeenth-century farmhouse also with strong Arts and Crafts associations, where the artist lived for fifteen years. Davies must have met many of the architects and craftsmen of the movement who lived in the area, in particular Norman Jewson who had restored the farmhouse. During the early years of the century amateur theatricals and puppet shows became a popular annual activity at Oakridge. Many literary friends spent weekends there, among them John Galsworthy, W.B. Yeats and Henry Newbolt. Rothenstein wrote in his memoirs:

> I would take them to remote valleys, through flowering orchards and hanging beechwoods, yet they never seemed to notice anything. Yeats would keep his eyes on the ground, and while Davies was with us he would talk literary gossip and ask my opinion of this or that poet, whilst cuckoos sang and rainbows arched the valley.[16]

His comment is intriguing in view of Davies's lines in 'A Great Time': 'A rainbow and a cuckoo's song may never come together again, / May never come this side the tomb.' Either Rothenstein misjudged Davies, or he quietly stored up verse material without drawing public attention to it.

Max Beerbohm had rented Winstons Cottage at Oakridge during the First World War, but he was not a country-lover and after a brief stay near Stroud he returned to London. A later tenant at Winstons Cottage was John Drinkwater, another old friend who wrote at least one play there. Ananda Coomaraswamy, an Anglo-Sri Lankan architect, had been educated at Wycliffe College near Stroud and formed part of the Gloucestershire Arts and Crafts community. Davies must have met many of this group when he visited the home of Claude

Biddulph at Rodmarton Manor, designed by Ernest Barnsley, built by Norman Jewson and Sidney Barnsley and completed in 1929 shortly after Davies's arrival in Nailsworth. So for a decade or so the area north and west of Stroud became a kind of rural Chelsea, which is likely to have influenced Davies when he decided to move westwards in middle age.

There was not a great deal of public entertainment on offer for the Davieses in Nailsworth between the wars, given that he had been a devotee of the theatre as a young man. As old friends died and others moved away from the Cotswolds Davies's circle of acquaintance narrowed to those who lived only a few miles away. Possibly it was Helen who discouraged visits to London, which could have been reached easily by train. They could attend an occasional concert in Bath or at the Stroud Subscription Rooms or else see a film at the Empire Cinema (opened in 1932 and later renamed the Odeon). Both Bath and Cheltenham were easily reached by car for shopping, and possibly Helen took advantage of any lifts she was offered.

Davies meanwhile was content with an occasional trip to see friends in London. Otherwise Nailsworth apparently satisfied him. Long-term elderly residents recall him stumping around the town, pipe or newspaper in hand. Mrs Elsie Sparrow, born in 1912, remembered him as a pleasant man in a tweed suit; although no inhabitant of the town from that era had done more than greet him with a good-day. What surprised some locals was the fact that his last home, Glendower, was a mile up a steep hill from the town centre. As they said, a man with one leg could hardly have chosen a more inconvenient house. However, it was the view and the quietness that appealed to Davies. A few years earlier Watledge had been noisier, with a joinery and undertakers' yard near by and a girls' school even closer; but during the period that the couple lived there the lane had turned into a desirable residential area. What very much irritated the poet, however, was that a previous resident had built a house directly opposite, cutting Glendower off from the best view across the valley. He believed that there was an element of personal malice in this.

Osbert Sitwell, in the foreword to a 1943 collection of Davies poems, told the story of the poet's pet toad which became a local legend.[17] He called it Jim and fed it milk, and to this day some people

believe a stone toad squats in the undergrowth of the Glendower garden. It has never been found, but a pug dog and a cat carved in stone,
almost certainly Davies's, have been uncovered beneath the bushes.

His poetic output slowed down during the Nailsworth years. In
this time Jonathan Cape published two sets of *Collected Poems* (updat-
ing the collection from time to time) and nine small books of
previously unpublished verse. A small Montgomeryshire company,
Gregynog Press at Newtown, in 1928 brought out *Selected Poems*,
chosen by Edward Garnett (the friend who had been instrumental in
getting Davies his Civil List pension) and *The Lover's Song Book*. In
the same year was published a handsome Medici Society limited
edition of forty-nine poems selected and illustrated by the artist
Jacynth Parsons. Her highly individual etchings represent the god Pan
as a willow tree and elsewhere depict a poet and a kingfisher by a
stream. In their fantasy and romance they accord well with the lyri-
cism of Davies's later verse. The artist was only seventeen when she
undertook the series of illustrations.

In 1934 a further distinction was conferred on Davies. The first
biography of him was published by the author and literary critic
Thomas Moult in a short series on modern writers which included
James Joyce and George Moore. For the most part Moult merely produced a commentary on Davies's better-known writings, but in his
final chapter he reproduced parts of an interview with the poet in the
garden of his Nailsworth home, and this gives insight into Davies's
writing technique. He said to Moult: 'You ask me how I write. Well,
there you are! I wait for a thought, an idea. I never make any attempt
to write until it comes to me – I simply go on with this quiet country
life, content to wait . . . Not always, of course, does a thought lead to a
complete lyric.' He chose as an example the word 'pock', as applied to
the effect of birds pecking at apples. Although the printer might
change pock to pick, for Davies 'the magic of the right word' was all-
important. Moult asked whether living in the country provided much
inspiration, to which he replied that ideas might come to him only
once a week but that he would be satisfied to write a poem a week –
less in summer. He found no need to keep a notebook; some poems
might be jotted down in a few minutes, unrevised.

Davies was emphatic that he did not regard himself as a nature poet. 'It wasn't long before they [the critics] were surprised into saying "What shall we do with this man Davies, whom we dismissed as a mere nature poet? Why, he can write other kinds of poetry as well!" . . . My philosophical verses convey no cribbed, cabined and confined view of life. A poet's moods change so often – and if they did not, it would be a case of farewell to poetry!'[18]

Another instance of Davies's recognition in his native Wales was the unveiling of a plaque at his birthplace on 21 September 1938 – the day that the Czech government resigned before Hitler's troops marched into Czechoslovakia. The local paper devoted two pages to the occasion, heading its report 'Where the Walls Have Diamond Eyes'. The first paragraph ran: 'Famous poet and author William Henry Davies returned to Newport to be honoured by his own folk, and among those who cheered him were some who remembered his father.' A second article in the newspaper was headed 'Tramp Poet of Gwent to Be Honoured by His County'.[19]

For the occasion Davies travelled to Newport by train with Helen and the Poet Laureate, John Masefield, who, despite their earlier coolness, had become a personal friend through the Sitwells. A civic party greeted him at the station and he was driven to the Church House Inn in Portland Street, the street not yet damaged by wartime bombing. At that time the Church House was flourishing as a a a public house and small shop. A blue plaque with the words 'Wm. Henry Davies, Poet & Author, born here 1871' (later they added 'Died 1940') replaced the conventional inn sign (after the war a new inn sign was designed to appear next to the plaque, bearing a striking portrait head of Davies, based on the Epstein bust, as its centrepiece). The plaque was unveiled by the Lady Mayor, and another local dignitary made a speech declaring that Davies's verse was known, loved and appreciated wherever the English language was spoken and understood. A press photograph from the *South Wales Argus* shows Davies looking rather embarrassed next to his more lofty companions, including John Masefield, with Helen standing inconspicuously in the background. After the ceremony there was a civic lunch at the Westgate Hotel, with speeches and the presentation of an inscribed half-grandfather clock from the people of Newport. This is the clock still standing in Glendower.

By 1940 Davies was unwell. He had had a stroke and, moreover, was much disturbed by the increasingly depressing war news. In May came the evacuation from Dunkirk, in late summer the Battle of Britain, and in the autumn began the so-called Baedeker raids, a series of massive bomber attacks on British cities – among them Bath, barely twenty miles from Nailsworth. In a poem called 'Armed for War' he wrote in distress of 'the baby, three weeks old, that wears a gas-proof mask' and 'the infant armed to meet a poisoned earth and sky'.

Another hint of air-raid horrors to come appears in 'Cherries', a section of *My Garden:* 'For over two hours, before midnight and after, the air above my house and garden has been filled with aircraft, and the sound of their machines has made sleep impossible . . . Is it with the eye of a prophet that I see the quiet heavens full of life, where strange monsters roar, tumble and glide by day and night?' Apart from this Davies left no record of his reaction to the events of the Second World War; as indeed he had written little about the First World War, save for tributes to friends who had died. War and politics were not his subjects; his writing was essentially personal, concerned with nature, aspects of society and the people he met.

His last collection of verse, *The Loneliest Mountain and Other Poems*, was published in 1939. In the preface Davies wrote: 'My doctor advises that the only hope of prolonging my life is to become lazy and selfish. But, whatever happens, the present book ends my career as a living author.'

A copy of the poems with a note in Davies's handwriting has this inscription:

> My book, W.H. Davies, Oct. 1939.
> The loneliest mountain, with no house or tree,
> Still has its little flower so sweet and wild,
> While I, a dreamer, strange and but half known,
> Can find no equal till I meet a child.
> W.H.D.[20]

A month later *My Garden and My Birds* appeared in one volume, the last of some fifty publications during his lifetime.

By late 1940 his health was failing (he had another mild stroke and heart problems) and he was not well enough to accept a dinner invitation from Violet Gordon Woodhouse to meet his old friends Edith and Osbert Sitwell. So his friends drove over to Nailsworth instead. To Osbert he confided in private that the pain was so great he 'would like to turn over on his side and die'.[21]

And he died very soon after this, at home with Helen, on 26 September 1940, when the Battle of Britain was at its height. Some Nailsworth inhabitants remember hearing the announcement of his death on a BBC radio news programme otherwise concerned with the day's total of enemy fighters shot down.

He was not buried at Nailsworth Parish Church but cremated at Cheltenham. Of the immediate family Helen attended the service; and Davies's nephew Noel Phillips, his wife and young sons came by taxi from Reading, petrol for private cars being virtually unobtainable at this time. Violet's Nether Lypiatt household was represented by her husband Gordon and the other surviving member of the original *mènage à cinq*, Lord Barrington. Apologies came from other writers who pleaded petrol shortages.

At that time cremation was still a novelty, and some have questioned Davies's religious beliefs. As an adult he did not follow the chapel-going practice in which he had been brought up, nor was he a church-goer. A single poem gives a clue to his belief. In 'Christ the Man' he disclaims all faith, but

> If knowledge is not great enough
> To give a man believing power,
> Lord, he must wait in Thy great hand
> Till revelation's hour
>
> . . .
>
> Meanwhile he'll follow Christ the man
> In that humanity he taught.

Tributes to him poured in, and almost every national newspaper carried an obituary, some written by then household names. Davies would have been gratified to read the accounts of his life by Desmond McCarthy, Richard Church and S.P.B. Mais and to note that his family connection with Sir Henry Irving was not overlooked.

One of the most detailed and perceptive posthumous portraits of Davies is given in Osbert Sitwell's *Noble Essences.* Sitwell wrote of the mingling of simplicity and intricacy in his character (compare this with Church's comment that he had a poet's naivety but a peasant's shrewdness). The artist Nina Hamnett, who had originally introduced Davies to the Sitwells, had informed them of his idiosyncratic rules for addressing people and being addressed by them. If he liked someone he would quickly start calling him or her by that person's Christian name but insisted that he himself was to remain 'Davies'. Eventually male friends would be allowed to call him William, but to women he must continue to be referred to as 'Mr Davies'.[22] Sitwell points out that this is consistent with his uneasiness with married women. Apparently when he met someone for the first time the poet would survey them with his head on one side, birdlike – 'with the same benevolent but appraising glance . . . whatever their standing might be in the eyes of the rest of the world'. When he had assessed his new acquaintance Davies would make some wry remark delivered in his Welsh accent. It was characteristic of the man that others were never quite sure whether he was laughing at them or whether he was slightly offended by some reaction. A lack of self-confidence underlay most of his initial social contacts, modified only when he knew people well.

Helen Thomas was one who knew him best outside his immediate circle, and her pen portrait written for *The Times* twenty years after his death rings true:

> Davies, for all his naïveté, was no simpleton. He had a Welshman's shrewdness in his sizing up of people's attitudes to him. Nor was he taken in by flattery, and when rich and fashionable people invited him to their houses and showed him off at their dinner parties, he knew full well that such things were not a tribute to his genius, but that their interest in the poet-cum-tramp would be very short-lived. And so it was.
>
> To our children he was always Sweet William, and he remained our dear and delightful friend until Edward left for France.[23]

In a way Davies provided his own obituary, for his final entry in

Who's Who bears all the hallmarks of having been written by him:

> Litt. D. Univ. of Wales; Poet and Author . . . picked up knowledge
> among tramps in America, on cattle boats, and in the common lodg-
> ing-houses in England . . . became a tramp in America; during tramp
> days, which lasted six years, picked fruit occasionally, and made eight
> or nine trips with cattle to England; came back to England and settled
> in common lodging-houses in London; made several walking tours as a
> pedlar of laces, pins and needles; sometimes varied this life by singing
> hymns in the street; after eight years of this published his first book of
> poems; became a poet at 34 years of age; been one ever since.

Then followed a list of thirty-eight publications. His recreation was
given as 'walking, mostly alone' and his address simply as Nailsworth,
Glos.[24] No mention was made of his traumatic experience in Canada,
his autobiography and many writings which were not poems, of his
fame as a portrait sitter, nor even, strangely, of his marriage. It was as
a poet that he wished to be remembered. In the twenty-first century
his fame as a poet rests largely on one poem out of more than seven
hundred.

1940 and After

This book is a human document . . . It cannot be said that I was born to the life of literary people. Indeed I seemed so far away from it that it appeared much more natural to seek a wife among the kind of people I knew before I was thirty years of age than the ones I knew later.

– Davies's introduction to his novel *Young Emma*, written 1924, published 1980

AFTER her husband's death Helen sold Glendower and moved to a flat in Bournemouth. It was a pleasant enough home in a between-wars redbrick house at 5 Queens Park Road, although it is not clear why she chose this seaside town. Acquaintances who knew her in those years have said she was not very well off; the royalties from her husband's work were not very significant, and at some stage the surviving letters and manuscripts in her possession were sold at auction to the University of Texas at Austin. It is unclear how many of the couple's other possessions were retained by her until her death, although she gave a neighbour, Betty Parker, a silver cruet as a gift.

Helen died in Bournemouth in 1979, nearly forty years after her husband. And then began a series of extraordinary events involving Helen's will, the publication of a hitherto unknown novel by her husband and the disinheriting of Davies's nearest surviving relatives.

In her will Helen left everything to Peter Flavell, a grandson of Louis Wixey the chemist who had made up prescriptions for the Davieses in Nailsworth. Peter's mother Nora, the second of Louis Wixey's four daughters, married a Midlands headmaster, John Flavell, and they had three children, of whom Peter, born in 1934, was the eldest. The will had been drafted six months after the poet's death and was never changed. After Louis died in 1948 the Wixey family had moved away, and Peter Flavell, by the time of Helen's death a middle-aged university librarian, was traced through an advertisement placed by solicitors in the *Birmingham Post*. As a boy Peter had lived in Birmingham with his parents, brother and sister, and during the war they stayed briefly with an aunt and uncle in Nailsworth.

To this day Peter Flavell, now retired from the University of Kent and living in Canterbury, has no clear idea why he was made Helen's heir. He has written:

> Helen Davies stipulated that I should receive all the income, that is, the royalties from her estate, while the capital should, on my death, be divided between my children. Should I die without issue then my brother Michael would inherit everything. I now have two daughters and five grandchildren. What motivated her to act in such a whimsical fashion? . . . Was it a form of gratitude to my grandfather for prescribing pain-killing drugs for her ailing husband? Did my mother, an occasional poet herself, befriend her during our brief sojourn in Nailsworth? Was she determined to prevent her legacy from falling into another pair of hands? Was Helen captivated by the fair-haired blue-eyed boy whose birthday happened to fall on the same day as that of her late husband?[1]

He asks another question which no one has been able to answer. Had Davies in his will given instructions about what should happen to his books and manuscripts? Peter checked the inventory of Helen's possessions, drove to Nailsworth and agreed with Mrs Margery Phillips – Davies's niece – and her son the items he should have. He had already examined the books left by Helen: 'Her possessions indicated the straitened circumstances she had been living in during her last years.'

Altogether Peter collected seventy books, a treasure trove for any book-lover, among them early editions of most of the poet's books. A first edition of *The Autobiography of a Super-Tramp* and a copy of *The Soul's Destroyer* were missing, assumed to have been given away long before Davies married Helen. There were several limited edition copies and private press publications, among them a set of *Raptures* printed on Japanese vellum. There were also sixteen manuscripts, mainly copies of previously published poems written out in Davies's small, meticulous hand, many of them with an inscription to his wife.

Some twelve months after her death came the publication of *Young Emma*, heralded by virtually every national newspaper and literary journal; copyright was vested in the estate of Mrs H.M. Davies. Peter has benefited from this as from the other royalties. He says: 'I would dearly have liked to have met Helen again. Perhaps she took a fancy to the small boy she saw once or twice in Nailsworth, when my family stayed there to escape the bombs in Birmingham. I think my mother was friendly with Helen through my Aunt Marjorie' (that same Marjorie who delivered prescriptions to the Davies house). It is of course possible that Helen felt indebted to the Wixey family for their professional kindness to her husband.

As a lover of books Peter was delighted to inherit so many of Davies's published works and the brown-covered exercise books. In each book the author had added the date, his address at the time (nine different ones appear) and his signature, usually Bunny but once Billy. Gradually Peter added more early publications, building up an almost complete collection of the poet's work which is probably unique in this country. Commenting on the generally held view that the later works are on the whole inferior, Peter says: 'When his muse was drying up and he was not in good health he rather ran out of ideas.'

Peter Flavell also owns a red leather album presented to the poet 'by a company of his admirers' during the luncheon held in his honour on 30 October 1930 at the Westgate Hotel in Newport. The illuminated front page states: 'These friends, whose names are inscribed herein, desire to express their pride in him as a Poet, and are grateful for the lasting contribution he has made to English Literature.' The first signatures are those of the Mayor and Mayoress, and the book includes pictures of local scenes. In response Davies read his favourite poem, 'Days That Have Been', a tribute to his native town.

Apart from the half-grandfather clock presented on this occasion, another memento of the poet – apart from the books – reached Peter. He treasures a small fob watch set in a miniature silver skull; the jaws of the skull open to reveal the watch – a novelty which would have appealed to Davies – and it carries the inscription 'Fugit Irreparabile Tempus'. His reaction to his inheritance and to all the later publicity about the novel *Young Emma*, which initially brought him £2,000 in royalties, has been astonishment.[2]

As we have seen, *Young Emma* was written soon after Davies married Helen, but the manuscript remained hidden away in the offices of his publishers, Jonathan Cape, for fifty-five years. The historian C.V. Wedgwood tells the story of its publication in her introduction to the novel. In 1924 Davies wrote to Cape about 'a new book I am writing;

another human document, so much so that it will have to be published under the name "Anonymous" '.[3] The book fills in the gaps of a similar account in *Later Days*.

As he described her in Chapter 5, Davies's central character was a young countrywoman who had come to London, became pregnant by an army officer who would not marry her and was turning to prostitution as a way out of poverty. The narrator, searching the London streets for a young woman who might agree to be his housekeeper-companion, met her at a bus stop near Marble Arch. He took pity on her and gave her a home, not knowing she was six months pregnant until she had to be rushed to hospital with a miscarriage. It took all night to find a hospital which would take her in, and the writer vividly conveys their fear and despair. While the woman was convalescing the narrator fell in love with her but hesitated to suggest marriage as he believed that she had given him venereal disease. This proved to be not the case, and when they both had recovered they happily set up home together in the country.

Although their real names are never given, the book was clearly autobiographical, depicting the early relationship of Helen and Davies. Jonathan Cape was reluctant to publish it as he believed that it would damage Davies's reputation. George Bernard Shaw supported this view, pointing out that Helen could be identified. 'If they were both dead it would be another matter,' he wrote in November 1924.[4]

At this stage Davies lost his nerve and asked Jonathan Cape to destroy the manuscript. Helen had heard about it and was alarmed. He went further and asked for written confirmation that two typed copies also had been destroyed: 'A book that is not fit to be published now can never be fit.' Jonathan Cape replied, sending Davies the original manuscript by registered post so that he could recycle elements of it in other works but postponing the destruction of the typed copies 'in case you might on reflection feel that to destroy everything is a little too drastic'. As far as is known, Davies did not inquire about the eventual fate of the two copies, which were locked away in a safe at the publishing house.

Eighteen years later the historian Veronica Wedgwood was working for Cape as a publisher's reader and was shown the novel. She recognized its worth as a social document, as a portrait of London after the First

World War, as well as a good novel. It was agreed that nothing could be done while Helen Davies was still alive. In 1972 the draft was resurrected, again praised by experts and again put away. Wedgwood succinctly puts the arguments for and against destroying it: to preserve it would be to ignore the wishes of both Davieses, but to destroy it would be an act of literary vandalism. She also wondered whether, subconsciously, since he never asked about it, Davies had hoped that the manuscript might survive.[5]

Whatever the ethics, in November 1980 Jonathan Cape finally published the novel. Indeed it is hard to imagine that any publisher would have done otherwise. Here was a fascinating and romantic autobiographical story (no one believed it to be wholly fiction) by an author still popular and widely read; a kind of sequel to *The Autobiography of a Super-Tramp*.

Its publication caused quite a stir. Ten years afterwards, and fifty years after the death of Davies, Tom Maschler, director of Jonathan Cape, was asked on BBC Radio 4 about the justification for bringing it out. He pointed out that there were precedents; authors often said 'Don't publish' but later changed their minds. The interviewer suggested that it was dishonest to fail to reveal that the manuscript had been kept; to which Maschler replied that Davies's instructions had been ambiguous. Much depended on the quality of the book, and this was a great love story, beautifully written. Although Davies was a very kind man, his attitude towards women was ambivalent. 'We did the world at large a service in drawing attention to a unique writer.' Asked if *Young Emma* should be regarded as autobiography or novel Maschler said it could be read either way. He said that Davies was a great man and that his writing had purity – for example, in a line such as 'trees thin and bare as robins' legs'.[6]

The *Sunday Times* successfully serialized part of *Young Emma* in 1980. As a novel it has some merit; as a social record, however, it is particularly remarkable. In the wake of *Young Emma* the autobiography and some of the poetry enjoyed a revival. Davies's verse appeared in poetry collections, broadcasts and magazine articles.

Throughout the twentieth century his poems have featured in anthologies. One in particular, the Methuen *Anthology of Modern Verse*, had a particularly distinguished pedigree. It was chosen by Alec

Methuen, with an introduction by Robert Lynd, and was dedicated to Thomas Hardy. It appeared in no fewer than sixty editions – many for schools – between 1921 and 1941. Included in it are seven of Davies's poems ('Where She Is Now', 'Leisure', 'The Kingfisher', 'Rich Days', 'A Great Time', 'Early Spring' and 'The Moon'), more than those of any other poet in the anthology except de la Mare, Yeats and Hardy himself.

Robert Lynd wrote in his introduction:

> To read him [Davies] is to see with new eyes, to hear with new ears. He invites us to a more intense experience than we have before known. Like Mr de la Mare, he bids us look on all things lovely as longingly as though it were for the last time ('A rainbow and a cuckoo's song / May never come together again'). Perhaps, however . . . Mr Davies has a gift for making us look at them for the first time. When we read his poem on the robin, 'That little hunchback in the snow', we feel as if we had never perfectly seen a robin before . . . Great poetry is not the expression of collective feeling. It is the speech of soul to soul.

Later Lynd praised Davies even more extravagantly. 'Mr Bridges and Mr Hardy, Mr Yeats and Mr Davies have all been the subjects of widely different estimates. [They] may well be content to know that they are luminaries for all time.'[7] In the case of Davies time has modified that judgement, and some major modern anthologies do not include his work at all. However, several distinguished recent poets have accorded Davies serious attention, among them Philip Larkin.

Larkin wrote in a 1963 *Guardian* article, 'Freshly Scrubbed Potato', that Davies was a literary curiosity who became a literary celebrity and finally part of literature itself. One or two of Larkin's perceptions of Davies are surprising: he observes that he was never more at home than when partying or lunching in London arts society, but 'domestic pressure forced him to give up most of his friends and live in the country, a region which he found he rather disliked as a permanent thing'. About Davies's verse Larkin was somewhat ambivalent, deeming some of it formulaic, mannered and stodgy but acknowledging the poet's power 'to refresh the commonest experience'. The metaphor of a scrubbed potato arises because Davies's poetry was not what might be expected of one who had led a picaresque lifestyle. 'His realism was that of the freshly scrubbed potato as opposed to the genuine earthy article (the image is Robert Frost's).'[8]

Larkin analysed the contrasts between Davies's companions when he was a hobo and those of literary London. 'Davies was not fastidious; he liked drinking and cheap whores, but there was an instinctive gentleness and adaptability about him that made him socially "possible" and facilitated his patronage by London literary society.' He admired Davies's tenderness towards animals, his love of children, natural surroundings, women, the poor – 'that this in its turn could come perilously close to kindergarten banality Davies was very well aware . . . his unique contribution to literature – a steady unecstatic celebration of natural beauty and the qualities in man that seem most allied to it'.

Another eminent poet who had a regard for Davies was Dylan Thomas, who included Davies in his series on Welsh poets, broadcast by the BBC in January 1946. After a brief résumé of his life Thomas said: 'His poems were always fresh and simple and assured. There was inevitability in his slightest verses; unique observation in his tiniest reflections on the natural world.' Thomas went on to explain why he had chosen to read two of Davies's more unfamiliar poems, to show him in a light 'no less loving than that in which his kingfishers, his robin-redbreasts, the little hunchbacks in the snow, all the inhabitants of his small and pure world move about their mysterious errands in the sky and on the earth he so much loved'. The poems Thomas chose were the macabre 'The Inquest', on the death of a four-month-old baby, perhaps by infanticide; and 'The Bust', retelling the story of a housekeeper who kept clean the lips of her lover's bust by kissing them. The quality Thomas sought to commend in both poems was a bizarre form of love. But what the listener remembers from his broadcast was his delight at Davies's skill in conveying 'the journeying of the planets and the seasons, the adventure of the coming and going of simple night and day'.[9]

Another popular Welsh broadcaster, Wynford Vaughan Thomas, read several Davies poems in public during the poet's lifetime. He was later to become a distinguished war correspondent. And Robert

Gittings, Francis Meynell, Edith Sitwell, Richard Church, John Arlott, Patric Dickinson and a number of leading actors were others who broadcast or presented his work.

In 1985 the novelist Margaret Drabble edited a comprehensively revised *Oxford Companion to English Literature* with a 22-line entry about Davies, briefly summarizing his life and naming four of his works as particularly noteworthy. It is no surprise to find listed *The Autobiography of a Super-Tramp* and the *Complete Poems* of 1963, with Osbert Sitwell's introduction. But less expected is the enthusiastic mention of *The Soul's Destroyer* and *Young Emma*.

The *New Oxford Book of English Verse*, edited by Helen Gardner and published in 1972, includes a typical choice of four poems – 'The Kingfisher', 'Leisure', 'The Inquest' and – more originally – 'The Cat' in which the poet expresses a comical fear of cats encountered at night:

> I cannot sleep if one is near;
> And though I'm sure I see those eyes
> I'm not so sure a body's there!

Another aspect of Davies's posthumous fame is the extent to which he may have influenced writers who came after him. David Taylor, biographer of George Orwell,[10] is convinced that *Down and Out in Paris and London* and *The Road to Wigan Pier* have echoes of the *Autobiography*. He argues that Orwell followed the same route as Davies through the seedier parts of London, staying in similar doss-houses in dockland and having similar encounters. An important difference between the two men is that Orwell was never genuinely homeless or penniless; rather, he was seeking raw material for his writings on Europe's underclass.[11]

Taylor makes a number of connections between the two authors, for instance, their shared obsession with rats. Davies developed his neurosis while sleeping rough in the USA, and its persistence was marked by his habit of putting out saucers of milk to placate imagined rodents even when living comfortably in Bloomsbury. Davies's poem 'The Rat', published in the collection *Nature* in 1914, describes a rat nibbling at a woman's corpse:

Now with these teeth that powder stones,
I'll pick at one of her cheek-bones:
When husband, son and daughter come,
They'll soon see who was left at home.

In this poem perhaps lay the origins of Winston Smith's torture by rats and of Orwell's concern with the rodents in several of his major books. Indeed in 1943 Orwell mentioned 'The Rat' in an *Observer* review of Davies's *Collected Poems*; although his own horrified fascination with the creatures seems to have developed, too, out of his experiences in Burma and in Spain.[12]

Not far from Nailsworth, across the Severn at Lydney in the Forest of Dean, lives a retired engineer whose passion is collecting early editions, manuscripts, posters and other memorabilia of Davies. Jim Riches discovered the poet when he was a schoolboy ('the only one I liked at school') and became a collector after he found a first edition in a job lot bought by a bookseller. The collection grew, and today he has early editions of all the books bar one and a number of associated books. He particularly values a manuscript article which he believes may never have been published. Davies wrote it in 1927 for the magazine *To-day*,[13] and it is extraordinarily revealing about his boyhood. Another valued book is a first edition of *The Hour of Magic* signed both by the poet and by the artist William Nicholson.

At the University of Texas at Austin there is a sizeable Davies archive which includes the signed original script of the essay 'My Memory of Edward Thomas'. This is meticulously written on six sheets of plain paper. In it he discusses Thomas's non-aggressiveness, the fact that Robert Frost persuaded him to switch from prose to poetry, their lunch and tea parties in Soho with literary friends. Davies's final comment expresses surprise that before the war Thomas could not get any poems accepted – to which was added in another hand 'How quickly these editors have changed their minds!' The collection also includes a number of manuscript versions of single poems ('How Kind Is Sleep', 'Joy Supreme', 'Laughing Rose', 'My Youth' and 'Young Beauty', among others) and several letters written to Davies by eminent authors. Among these is a letter from Thomas Hardy dated 1919 and another from Edmund Blunden in 1921, as well as a series from Edward Garnett written between 1894 and 1928. The university also holds what may be the only copy of the statement by W.H. Hudson in support of Edward Garnett's petition for a Civil List pension for Davies and Joseph Conrad's supporting note.[14] There are handwritten reviews of Davies's poems by A.E. Coppard and H.M. Tomlinson – this last found in a collection of letters from Tomlinson to Siegfried Sassoon.

Preserved in the Harry Ransom Humanities Research Center at Austin, Texas, are letters from Davies to two of his publishers, Alfred Knopf and Jonathan Cape, which show him to be more businesslike than might be supposed. He makes precise arrangements about meetings, payments for pictures and corrected proofs. Other archive material held there includes printed Davies works signed by their owners; but none shows evidence that they were given to them personally by Davies. There is in fact a sizeable market for Davies archive material.

The poet would be entertained to learn that his verse has even featured on television – a medium still in its infancy when he died. In 2001 a chain of outdoor holiday centres, Center Parcs, commissioned an television advertisement with a voice-over reading some lines from 'Leisure'. The title of the poem and the author's name appeared above as a caption. The advertisements ran for some weeks until 2002. What troubled some aficionados of Davies was that the poem was read by a man with a broad Scots accent. Asked why a Welsh actor had not been chosen, the advertising agency concerned said that Welsh was not a fashionable accent. One can imagine Davies's reaction to this.

Nor is the poet forgotten in Nailsworth by the younger generation. To mark the fiftieth anniversary of his death schoolchildren presented a concert of Davies poems set to music for the occasion, entitled 'What Is This Life?' A wooden wall plaque of his head by a Stroud sculptor, David John, was set up in the local public library. Several years later, at Nailsworth Town Hall, a local theatre group gave an original presentation of *The Autobiography of a Super-Tramp* in drama, song and verse. They called it *Days That Have Been. A Stage Ballad: The Life and Times of W.H. Davies the Tramp Poet.* The town has a trail of landmarks associated with Davies, and in summer tourists ask after him.

Across the Severn Bridge in Newport in 1990 a modernist bronze sculpture inspired by the poem 'Leisure' was unveiled in the shopping centre. The more than lifesize figure, by Paul Bothwell Kincaid, shows a stylized veiled woman. An inscription set in paving stones around the statue reads: 'Stand and Stare'. After the unveiling ceremony the Mayor gave tea to guests in the town hall; among the guests was Davies's great-nephew Norman Phillips.

Newport is proud of its famous son. Apart from the street sculpture, the art gallery, the library and, most especially, the Church House Inn are places of pilgrimage. When Norman Phillips visited the sh in 2001, the walls of its bar decorated with Davies photographs and souvenirs, he met Margaret Reilly, who as a small girl, aged about five, appears in a photograph of the bystanders when the new inn sign was unveiled in 1938.[15] She is seated on her father's shoulders, not far from Davies himself. Regulars gathered in the bar, pleased to meet Norman and chat about the Davies connection with their pub. They believed that he had been born 'over where the lounge bar is now', and they knew that Mahoney's shop had adjoined the pub in the 1870s. Another reminder mentioned by regulars is a nearby pub, the Welsh Prince, named after the ferryboat that the boy William Henry sailed on across the Bristol Channel with his mariner grandfather Captain William Davies.

In Nailsworth tourists visit Glendower to to photograph the stone by the front door and to read the lines from 'Leisure' inscribed on it. The cottage is a listed building, sadly neglected, which the district council plans to help Norman Phillips restore. He intends to leave it to a nephew.

In 1996 BBC television conducted a poll to learn which were listeners' favourite poems. Some 12,000 voted Kipling's 'If' into first place, followed by Tennyson's 'The Lady of Shalott' and third 'The Listeners' by Davies's old friend Walter de la Mare. 'Leisure' came in at number fourteen, after his fellow-Welshman Dylan Thomas ('Fern Hill') but ahead of Andrew Marvell ('To His Coy Mistress'), Matthew Arnold ('Dover Beach') and William Blake ('The Tyger').[16] There is a certain irony in the fact that Edward Thomas, who did so much to launch Davies as a poet and befriend him, was voted no higher than twentieth, with 'Adlestrop', followed by Rupert Brooke's 'The Soldier', while the twenty-seventh place was taken by 'Cargoes' – one of two poems by John Masefield. Thomas, Brooke and Masefield still stand high in that pantheon of writers whose company had delighted Davies before the First World War and during the 1920s.

Commercials and popularity polls are not the only media through which Davies's verse is celebrated today. In the summer of 2003 a garden designed by prisoners at Leyhill, an open prison in Gloucestershire, a few miles from his Nailsworth home, won a gold medal at Chelsea Flower Show, the most prestigious show of its kind in the world. Its theme was the poem 'Leisure'. Millions saw the garden on television or came in person to look at it. It conveyed powerfully an atmosphere of contemplation and calm, with wild plants, a very natural-looking artificial lake and a picturesque old wooden boat. All this would have appealed enormously to Davies, with his love of wildlife, gardens and boats.

There is a certain irony in the fact that, givenl his prolific output, he is remembered today mainly for *The Autobiography of a Super-Tramp*, for *Young Emma* and for one poem out of the many hundreds he published in his lifetime.

He manifested an odd mixture of characteristics: vain but shy, self-important but insecure. Such contrast appears, too, in his writings. He mainly confined himself to a meditative, even bucolic view of life: focusing on his travels, his response to nature and to the people and places he had encountered. Yet several of the poems illustrate a world filled with malaise or misery, violence or even horror, as in 'The Soul's Destroyer'. His autobiographical writings generally suggest a relaxed, philosophical approach to life, yet a darker vision and a preoccupation with death break through in works such as *Later Days* and *Young Emma*.

Davies himself grouped his work broadly into four categories under the headings nature, philosophy, love and religion. Religion is the least obviously apparent of his themes, but sensitive readers will be aware of his sense of an underlying purpose in the scheme of things, as when he reflects on poverty, the symbolism of birds or the generosity of good men, and in 'Christ the Man' he explicitly acknowledges a moral and spiritual influence. Davies was a Blakean observer of the natural universe, sometimes seeing the world in a grain of sand and always heaven in a wild flower.

Notes

Chapter 1: Victorian Newport and Nailsworth

1. Haydn Davis, *History of the Borough of Newport*, Pennyfarthing Press, Newport, 1998, p. 130.
2. 'The Child and the Mariner', from *Collected Poems*, Jonathan Cape, London, 1916, p. 154.
3. Lawrence Hockey, *Writers of Wales: W.H. Davies*, University of Wales Press, Cardiff, 1971, p. 4.
4. 'A Poet's Alphabet' in *Complete Poems*, Jonathan Cape, London, 1963, p. 359.
5. 'The Child and the Mariner', *Collected Poems*, 1916, p. 154.
6. Hockey, pp. 5–6.
7. *Monmouthshire Merlin*, 25 January 1884, p. 8.
8. *The True Traveller*, Duckworth, London, 1912, pp. 279–83.
9. 'A Stormscape', poem in *Monmouthshire Merlin*, 27 February 1887.
10. *The True Traveller*, p. 198.
11. Interview with Lawrence Hockey, BBC Radio 4, 20 December 1980.
12. Mentioned in *Beggars*, Duckworth, London, 1909, pp. 183–7.
13. *The True Traveller*, p. 1.
14. *Beggars*, p. 222.

Chapter 2: Down and Out in the USA

1. *A Poet's Calendar*, Jonathan Cape, London, 1927, p.57.
2. Information from Baltimore City Life Museums.
3. Jack London, *The Road* (1907), Macmillan, New York, pp. 43–4.
4. Tim Cresswell, *The Tramp in America*, Reaktion Books, London, 2001, Chapter 3.
5. *The Autobiography of a Super-Tramp*, Jonathan Cape, London, 1908, p. 80.
6. *Dancing Mad*, Jonathan Cape, London, 1927.
7. Cresswell, *The Tramp in America*, p.190.
8 Charles Chaplin Jr, *My Father, Charlie Chaplin*, Longmans Green and Co., London, 1960, p. 23.
9. 'A Tramp's Camp in Texas', in *Beggars*, pp. 12–18.
10. *The Autobiography of a Supertramp*, pp. 94–8.

11. In the private collection of Jim Riches of Lydney,
    Gloucestershire.
12. *Evening Standard, c.* 8 January 1899.

Chapter 3: Down and Very Much Out in Canada

1. *Evening Standard*, February/March 1899.
2. *The Adventures of Johnny Walker, Tramp*, Jonathan Cape, London, 1926,
   p. 77.
3. *Ibid.*, p. 82.
4. *The Autobiography of a Super-Tramp*, p. 161.
5. London, *The Road*.
6. Cresswell, *The Tramp in America*, Ch. 1.
7. Information about Renfrew from www.countyofrenfrew.on.ca.
8. *Renfrew Mercury*, 31 March 1899.
9. Personal communication from Carol Bennett McCuaig, author of *Renfrew
   Victoria Hospital 1897–1997*, Juniper Books, Toronto, 1997, and *In Search
   of the Red Dragon: The Welsh in Canada*, Juniper Books, Toronto, 1985.
10. Information supplied by Carol Bennett McCuaig and Sandy Buttle of
    Renfrew, Ontario.
11. *Renfrew Mercury*, 24 March 1899.
12. *The Autobiography of a Super-Tramp*, pp. 180–1.

Chapter 4: Struggling in Middle England

1. *The Autobiography of a Super-Tramp*, p. 196.
2. *The Adventures of Johnny Walker, Tramp*, p. 191.
3. *Ibid.*, p. 240.
4. 'How It Feels to Be Out of Work', *English Review*, 1908–9, Vol. 1, p. 169.
5. *The True Traveller*, p. 225.

Chapter 5: Becoming a Published Writer

1. Charles Dickens, *Little Dorrit*, Nelson Classics, London, *c.* 1935, p. 61.
2. *The Autobiography of a Super-Tramp*, pp. 285–6.
3. *Daily Mail*, 22 July 1905, p. 3.
4. *Later Days*, p. 138.
5. John Moore, *Life and Letters of Edward Thomas*, Heinemann, London,
   1939, p. 291.
6. *Ibid.*, p.141.

7. *The Odd Volume*, Simpkin, Marshall, Hamilton, Kent, London, 1910, pp. 5–16.

8. Helen Thomas, 'The Discovery of W.H. Davies', *The Times*, 27 March 1963, p. 12.

9. Myfanwy Thomas, personal communication.

10. Shaw's Preface to *The Autobiography of a Super-Tramp* (7th New English Edition, Jonathan Cape, London, 1946), p. 15.

11. *Later Days*, p. 65.

12. *Sevenoaks Chronicle*, 7 September 1951, p. 5.

13. Manuscript in possession of Sevenoaks Library, Kent; undated.

14. Private collection of Jim Riches of Lydney, Gloucestershire; dated 27 November, no year.

15. The manuscript in Jim Riches's possession seems not to have been corrected or edited.

16. *English Review*, 1 December 1908, pp. 168–71.

17. *The Odd Volume*, p. 14.

18. Archives of the Harry Ransom Humanities Research Center, University of Texas at Austin.

19. *New York Times*, 7 July 1911, p. 1.

20. All references in this chapter to Edward Marsh and Edward Gosse are taken from Christopher Hassall, *Edward Marsh: A Biography*, Longmans, London, 1959, pp. 206–9, 235, 366–7.

21. Eleanor Farjeon, *Edward Thomas: The Last Four Years*, Oxford University Press, Oxford, 1958, pp. 120, 175.

Chapter 6: London Literary Lions

1. *Later Days*, p. 112.

2. Handwritten letter in the Davies archive of the Harry Ransom Humanities Research Center, University of Texas at Austin.

3. *Later Days*, p. 152.

4. *Ibid.*, p. 55.

5. Edward Marsh, 'Memoir' in *Rupert Brooke: The Collected Poems*, Sidgwick and Jackson, London, 1918, p. 100.

6. Hassall, *Edward Marsh: A Biography*, p. 461.

7. *Ibid.*, pp. 286–7.

8. R.J. Stonesifer, *W.H. Davies*, Jonathan Cape, London, 1963, p. 55.

9. Osbert Sitwell, *Noble Essences*, Macmillan, London, 1950, p. 230.

10. Eleanor Farjeon, *Edward Thomas: The Last Four Years*, Oxford University Press, Oxford, 1979, p. 139.

11. Helen Thomas, 'The Discovery of W.H. Davies', *The Times*, 27 March 1963, p. 12.

12. *Later Days*, p.49.

13. Richard Church interviewed on BBC Radio Wales, February 1968.

14. Sitwell, *Noble Essences*, pp. 213–14.

15. *Ibid.*, p. 221.

16. Norman Jewson, *By Chance I Did Rove*, Macmillan, London, 1927, pp. 107–8.

17. *Later Days*, p. 258.

18. Stephen Gardiner, *Epstein*, Michael Joseph, London, 1992, pp. 165–71.

19. Augustus John, *Chiaroscuro*, Jonathan Cape, London, 1952, pp. 151–2.

20. Stonesifer, *W.H. Davies*, p. 127.

21. *Times Literary Supplement*, 12 October 1922, p. 651.

22. Laura Knight, interviewed on BBC Radio Wales, 1968.

23. *A Poet's Pilgrimage*, Andrew Melrose, London, 1918, pp. 281–3.

24. Sitwell, *Noble Essences*, p. 237

25. *Ibid.*, pp. 243–4.

26. Letter in the collection of Jim Riches of Lydney, Gloucestershire.

27. *Later Days*, pp. 72–4.

Chapter 7: Davies the Married Man

1. *Later Days*, Jonathan Cape, London, 1925, p. 216.??

2. *Young Emma*, Jonathan Cape, London, 1980, p. 22.

3. *Ibid.*, p. 31.

4. *Ibid.*, p. 55.

5. *Ibid.*, p, 119.

6. *Ibid.*, p. 136.

7. Biographies of Aiken and Armstrong in *Who Was Who*, 1971–1980, A. and C. Black, London, pp. 9, 27.

8. Stonesifer, *W.H. Davies*, p. 137.

9. Handwritten letter to Holbrook Jackson, undated, in the collection of Jim Riches, Lydney, Gloucestershire.

10. *Shorter Lyrics of the Twentieth Century*, ed. W.H. Davies, Poetry Bookshop, London, 1922.

11. 'My Memory of Edward Thomas', in *Voices in Poetry and Prose*, October

1920, pp. 118–22.

12. *The Fortunes and Misfortunes of the Famous Moll Flanders: A New Edition with an Introduction by W.H. Davies*, John Lane at the Bodley Head, London, 1929, pp. v–viii.

13. J.C. Squire, *Collected Parodies*, Hodder and Stoughton, London, 1921, pp. 36–7.

14. C. Henry Warren, 'Self-Portrait of a Poet', *The Bookman*, December 1925, pp. 179–80.

15. 'Poets and Critics', *New Statesman*, 8 September 1923, p. 543.

16. *A Poet's Calendar*, Jonathan Cape, London, 1927, p.35.

17. *Ibid.*, p. 49.

18. Introduction to *The Adventures of Johnny Walker, Tramp*, second edition, Jonathan Cape, London, 1932, p. 7.

19. *Ibid.*, p. 67.

Chapter 8: Nailsworth in the 1930s

1. Stonesifer, *W.H. Davies*, p. 150.

2. Examples are given in Peter Flavell's collection of early editions of W.H. Davies's books.

3. Personal communication.

4. Brian Waters, Preface to *The Essential W.H. Davies*, Jonathan Cape, London, 1951, p. 11.

5. *Ibid.*, p. 4.

6. Introduction to *The Fortunes and Misfortunes of the Famous Moll Flanders*, 1929, p. vii.

7. The title deeds of Glendower, in the possession of Norman Philips.

8. Waters, *The Essential W.H. Davies*, p. 2.

9. Laura Riding and Robert Graves, *A Survey of Modernist Poetry*, Heinemann, London, 1927, pp. 200–1.

10. 'Nation's Tribute: Honour to Whom Honour Is Due', *Western Mail*, 20 July 1929, pp. 1, 6.

11. Letter in the collection of Jim Riches of Lydney, Gloucestershire, dated 15 October 1930.

12. Information from BBC Sound Archives and Sylvia Harlow, *W.H. Davies: A Bibliography*, St Paul's Bibliographies, Oak Knoll Books, Delaware, 1993, pp. 174–9.

13. Jessica Douglas-Home, *Violet*, Harvill Press, London, 1996, p. 169.

14. Victoria Glendinning, *A Unicorn among Lions*, Weidenfeld and Nicolson, London, 1981, p. 57.

15. Edith Sitwell, *Selected Letters*, ed. Richard Greene, Virago, London, 1997, p. 141.

16. William Rothenstein, *Men and Memories*, Faber and Faber, London, 1932, Vol. II, p. 341.

17. Osbert Sitwell, Foreword to *Complete Poems of W.H. Davies*, Jonathan Cape, London, 1943, p. xxxiv.

18. Thomas Moult, *W.H. Davies*, Thornton Butterworth, London, 1934, pp. 137–44.

19. 'Where the Walls Have Diamond Eyes', *South Wales Argus*, 21 September 1938, pp. 6, 8.

20. Handwritten note on flyleaf of first edition of *The Loneliest Mountain*, Jonathan Cape, London, 1939 (book in the collection of Newport Public Library).

21. Sitwell, *Noble Essences*, p. 243.

22. Nina Hamnett, *Laughing Torso*, R. Long and R. Smith, London, 1932, p. 98.

23. Helen Thomas, 'The Discovery of W.H. Davies', p. 12.

24. *Who Was Who, 1929–1940*, A. and C. Black, London, p. 338.

Chapter 9: 1940 and After

1. Typescript of unpublished memoir by Peter Flavell.

2. Personal communication with Peter Flavell.

3. Quoted by C.V. Wedgwood in Foreword to *Young Emma*, p. 9.

4. George Bernard Shaw, letter to Jonathan Cape dated 8 November 1924, reproduced in appendix to *Young Emma*, p. 157.

5. C.V. Wedgwood, Foreword to *Young Emma*, p. 13.

6. Tom Maschler interviewed on BBC Radio 4 in 1990 on the occasion of the fiftieth anniversary of Davies's death.

7. Robert Lynd, Introduction to *An Anthology of Modern Verse*, Methuen, London, 1941, pp. xxiii, xxxiii.

8. Philip Larkin, 'Freshly Scrubbed Potato', *Required Writing: Miscellaneous Pieces, 1955–82*, Faber and Faber, London, 1983, pp. 164–7 (this article originally appeared in the *Guardian*).

9. Dylan Thomas, radio scripts collected in *Quite Early One Morning*, J.M. Dent, London, 1954, pp. 145–7 (first broadcast BBC Eastern

Service, 5 January 1946).

10. David Taylor, *Orwell: The Life*, Chatto and Windus, London, 2003, pp. 93, 143–4; also personal communication.

11. George Orwell, *Down and Out in Paris and London*, Gollancz, London, 1933, pp. 114–23.

12. George Orwell, *1984*, Secker and Warburg, London, 1949, pp. 246–9.

13. Manuscript in the collection of Jim Riches of Lydney, Gloucestershire; letter is presumed to be addressed to Holbrook Jackson, editor of *To-day*; undated but believed to have been written in 1927.

14. Typed statement in the collection of the Harry Ransom Humanities Research Center, University of Texas at Austin, written by W.H. Hudson with handwritten postscript by Joseph Conrad; undated but believed to have been written on 17 February 1911.

15. Photograph in *South Wales Argus*, 21 September 1938, p. 6.

16. *The Nation's Favourite Poems*, ed. G. Rhys Jones, BBC Worldwide, London, 1996, p. 32.

Bibliography

Works by W.H. Davies

POETRY

The Soul's Destroyer (Alston Rivers, London, 1907)

New Poems (Elkin Mathews, London, 1907)

Farewell to Poesy (A. C. Fifield, London, 1910)

Songs of Joy (A. C. Fifield, London, 1911)

Foliage (Elkin Mathews, London, 1913)

The Bird of Paradise (Methuen, London, 1914)

Nature (B.T. Batsford, London, 1914)

Child Lovers (A. C. Fifield, London, 1916)

A Poet's Pilgrimage (Andrew Melrose, London, 1918)

Raptures (Beaumont Press, London, 1918)

Forty New Poems (A. C. Fifield, London, 1918)

The Song of Life (A. C. Fifield, London, 1920)

The Captive Lion (Yale University Press, New Haven, 1921)

The Hour of Magic (Jonathan Cape, London, 1922)

Secrets (Jonathan Cape, London, 1924)

A Poet's Alphabet (Jonathan Cape, London, 1925)

The Song of Love (Jonathan Cape, London, 1926)

A Poet's Calendar (Jonathan Cape, London, 1927)

Moss and Feather (Faber and Gwyer, London, 1928)

Forty-nine Poems (Medici Society, London, 1928)

Ambition (Jonathan Cape, London, 1929)

Poems 1930–1931 (Jonathan Cape, London, 1932)

The Lovers' Song Book (Gregynog Press, Newtown, Montgomeryshire, 1933)

Love Poems (Jonathan Cape, London, 1935)

The Birth of Song (Jonathan Cape, London, 1936)

The Loneliest Mountain (Jonathan Cape, London, 1939)

PROSE

The Autobiography of a Super-Tramp (A.C. Fifield, London, 1908)

Beggars (Duckworth and Co., London, 1909)

A Weak Woman (Duckworth and Co., London, 1911)

The True Traveller (Duckworth and Co., London, 1912)

First American edition of *The Autobiography of a Super-Tramp* (Alfred A. Knopf, New York, 1917)

True Travellers: A Tramps Opera (Jonathan Cape, London, 1923)

Later Days (Jonathan Cape, London, 1925)

The Adventures of Johnny Walker, Tramp (Jonathan Cape, London, 1926)

Dancing Mad (Jonathan Cape, London, 1927)

My Birds (Jonathan Cape, London, 1933)

My Garden (Jonathan Cape, London, 1933)

Young Emma (Jonathan Cape, London, 1980)

Works edited by W.H. Davies

Shorter Lyrics of the Twentieth Century (Poetry Bookshop, London, 1922)

Form (four monthly issues) (Moreland Press, London, 1921)

Jewels of Song (Jonathan Cape, London, 1930)

An Anthology of Short Poems (Jonathan Cape, London, 1938)

BBC broadcasts (excluding repeats)

Reading fifteen of his own poems (London, 3 September 1924)

Discussion with Miles Malleson and Harold Monro (London, 3 December 1925)

Talk: 'The Rungs of the Ladder' (BB National, 16 May 1932)

Reading fifteen of his own poems (London, 1 December 1933)

Reading twenty of his own poems (BBC Wales, 20 September 1937)

Reading eleven of his own poems (Regional BBC, 5 February 1938)

'Time Turns Back: The Trial of William Shakespeare for Deer Stealing' (Midland Service, 2 May 1938)

Serialized reading of *The Autobiography of a Super-Tramp* (Regional Services, 16 October–22 November 1938)

Reading of 'Love Poetry by Dead Masters' (BBC National, 7 January 1939)

Reading five of his own poems (broadcast posthumously), Home Service and Forces Network, 26 September and 3 October, 1940

Selected Poems of W.H. Davies

Note: All except four of these poems were chosen by W.H. Davies when he was asked to broadcast some of his favourite poems between 1924 and 1938. He did not choose 'Leisure', the poem which has made him famous; and he did not read 'Sleepers', 'A Great Time' or 'The Bird of Paradise', although these have been broadcast by others in the years since his death.

The Moon (1905)

> Thy beauty haunts me heart and soul,
>   O thou fair Moon, so close and bright;
> Thy beauty makes me like the child,
>   That cries aloud to own thy light:
> The little child that lifts each arm,
> To press thee to her bosom warm.
>
> Though there are birds that sing this night
>   With thy white beams across their throats,
> Let my deep silence speak for me
>   More than for them their sweetest notes:
> Who worships thee till music fails,
> Is greater than thy nightingales.

The Kingfisher (1910)

It was the Rainbow gave thee birth,
   And left thee all her lovely hues;
And as her mother's name was Tears,
   So runs it in my blood to choose
For haunts the lonely pools, and keep
In company with trees that weep.

Go you and, with such glorious hues,
   Live with proud Peacocks in green parks;
On lawns as smooth as shining glass,
   Let every feather show its marks;
Get thee on boughs and clap thy wings
Before the windows of proud kings.

Nay, lovely Bird, thou art not vain;
   Thou hast no proud, ambitious mind;
I also love a quiet place
   That's green, away from all mankind;
A lonely pool, and let a tree
Sigh with her bosom over me.

The Sluggard (1910)

A jar of cider and my pipe,
 In summer, under shady tree;
A book of one that made his mind
 Live by its sweet simplicity:
Then must I laugh at kings who sit
 In richest chambers, signing scrolls;
And princes cheered in public ways,
 And stared at by a thousand fools.

Let me be free to wear my dreams,
 Like weeds in some mad maiden's hair,
When she doth think the earth has not
 Another maid so rich and fair;
And proudly smiles on rich and poor,
 The queen of all fair women then:
So I, dressed in my idle dreams,
 Will think myself the king of men.

Leisure (1911)

What is this life if, full of care,
We have no time to stand and stare.

No time to stand beneath the boughs
And stare as long as sheep or cows.

No time to see, when woods we pass,
Where squirrels hide their nuts in grass.

No time to see, in broad daylight,
Streams full of stars, like skies at night.

No time to turn at Beauty's glance,
And watch her feet, how they can dance.

No time to wait till her mouth can
Enrich that smile her eyes began.

A poor life this if, full of care,
We have no time to stand and stare.

Christ, the Man (1911)

Lord, I say nothing: I profess
   No faith in thee nor Christ thy Son:
Yet no man ever heard me mock
   A true believing one.

If knowledge is not great enough
   To give a man believing power,
Lord, he must wait in thy great hand
   Till revelation's hour.

Meanwhile he'll follow Christ, the man
   In that humanity he taught,
Which to the poor and the oppressed
   Gives its best time and thought.

Days That Have Been (1911)

Can I forget the sweet days that have been,
  When poetry first began to warm my blood;
When from the hills of Gwent I saw the earth
  Burned in two by Severn's silver flood:

When I would go alone at night to see
  The moonlight, like a big white butterfly,
Dreaming on that old castle near Caerleon,
  While at its side the Usk went softly by:

When I would stare at lovely clouds in Heaven,
  Or watch them when reported by deep streams;
When feeling pressed like thunder, but would not
  Break into that grand music of my dreams?

Can I forget the sweet days that have been,
  The villages so green I have been in;
Llantarnam, Magor, Malpas, and Llanwern,
  Liswery, old Caerleon, and Alteryn?

Can I forget the banks of Malpas Brook,
  Or Ebbw's voice in such a wild delight,
As on he dashed with pebbles in his throat,
  Gurgling towards the sea with all his might?

Ah, when I see a leafy village now,
  I sigh and ask it for Llantarnam's green;
I ask each river where is Ebbw's voice –
  In memory of the sweet days that have been.

The Sleepers (1911)

As I walked down the waterside
   This silent morning, wet and dark;
Before the cocks in farmyards crowed,
   Before the dogs began to bark;
Before the hour of five was struck
By old Westminster's mighty clock:

As I walked down the waterside
   This morning, in the cold damp air,
I saw a hundred women and men
   Huddled in rags and sleeping there:
These people have no work, thought I,
And long before their time they die.

That moment, on the waterside,
   A lighted car came at a bound;
I looked inside, and saw a score
   Of pale and weary men that frowned;
Each man sat in a huddled heap,
Carried to work while fast asleep.

Ten cars rushed down the waterside,
   Like lighted coffins in the dark;
With twenty dead men in each car,
   That must be brought alive by work:
These people work too hard, thought I,
And long before their time they die.

A Great Time (1914)

Sweet Chance, that led my steps abroad,
  Beyond the town, where wild flowers grow –
A rainbow and a cuckoo, Lord,
  How rich and great the times are now!
    Know, all ye sheep
    And cows that keep

On staring that I stand so long
  In grass that's wet from heavy rain –
A rainbow and a cuckoo's song
  May never come together again;
    May never come
    This side the tomb.

The Bird of Paradise (1914)

Here comes Kate Summers who, for gold
   Takes any man to bed:
'You know my friend, Nell Barnes,' said she;
   'You knew Nell Barnes – she's dead.

'Nell Barnes was bad on all you men,
   Unclean, a thief as well;
Yet all my life I have not found
   A better friend than Nell.

'So I sat at her side at last,
   For hours, till she was dead;
And yet she had no sense at all
   Of any word I said.

'For all her cry but came to this –
   "Not for the world! Take care:
Don't touch that bird of paradise,
   Perched on the bedpost there!"

'I asked her would she like some grapes,
   Some damsons ripe and sweet;
A custard made with new-laid eggs,
   Or tender fowl to eat.

'I promised I would follow her,
   To see her in her grave;
And buy a wreath with borrowed pence,
   If nothing I could save.

'Yet still her cry but came to this –
   "Not for the world! Take care:
Don't touch that bird of paradise,
   Perched on the bedpost there!"'

I Am the Poet Davies, William (1918)

I am the poet Davies, William,
    I sin without a blush or blink:
I am a man that lives to eat;
    I am a man that lives to drink.

My face is large, my lips are thick,
    My skin is coarse and black almost;
But the ugliest feature is my verse,
    Which proves my soul is black and lost.

Thank heaven thou didst not marry me,
    A poet full of blackest evil;
For how to manage my damned soul
    Will puzzle many a flaming devil.

Killed in Action (1918)

(*Edward Thomas*)

Happy the man whose home is still
  In Nature's green and peaceful ways;
To wake and hear the birds so loud,
  That scream for joy to see the sun
Is shouldering past a sullen cloud.

And we have known those days, when we
  Would wait to hear the cuckoo first;
When you and I, with thoughtful mind,
  Would help a bird to hide her nest,
For fear of other hands less kind.

But thou, my friend, art lying dead:
  War, with its hell-born childishness,
Has claimed thy life, with many more:
  The man that loved this England well,
And never left it once before.

Rich Days (1923)

Welcome to you rich Autumn days,
   Ere comes the cold, leaf-picking wind;
When golden stooks are seen in fields,
   All standing arm-in-arm entwined;
And gallons of sweet cider seen
On trees in apples red and green.

With mellow pears that cheat our teeth,
   Which melt that tongues may suck them in;
With blue-black damsons, yellow plums,
   Now sweet and soft from stone to skin;
And woodnuts rich, to make us go
Into the loneliest lanes we know.

A Child's Pet (1923)

When I sailed out of Baltimore,
   With twice a thousand head of sheep,
They would not eat, they would not drink,
   But bleated o'er the deep.

Inside the pens we crawled each day,
   To sort the living from the dead;
And when we reached the Mersey's mouth,
   Had lost five hundred head.

Yet every night and day one sheep,
   That had no fear of man or sea,
Stuck through the bars its pleading face,
   And it was stroked by me.

And to the sheep-men standing near,
   'You see,' I said, 'this one tame sheep?
It seems a child has lost her pet,
   And cried herself to sleep.'

So every time we passed it by,
   Sailing to England's slaughter-house,
Eight ragged sheep-men – tramps and thieves –
   Would stroke that sheep's black nose.

Index

friends near Nailsworth, 142, 148,
150–2; life during Second World
War, 155; final illness and death,
156

Daily Chronicle, 81

Daily Mail, 82

de la Mare, Walter, 86, 92, 102, 113,
128, 130

Defoe, Daniel, 143

'Detroit Fatty', 40

Dickens, Charles, 26, 79

Drabble, Margaret, 166

Drake, Peggy (née Wixey), 141

Drinkwater, John, 94, 151

Duckworth and Company, 84,
89–90

Dudbridge Donkey, 141

Dymock Group, 94

East Grinstead, 123, 125, 126, 128

Egg Pie Lane, 82

Eliot, T.S., 108, 116

Emperor of the North, The, 58

Empire Cinema, Stroud, 152

Epstein, Sir Jacob, 110–11

Evans, Mary Ann *see* Mary Ann
Davies

Evans, Gomer, 21, 25

Evan, Huw, 21

Evening Standard, 51–2

Farjeon, Eleanor, 95, 104

Farmhouse, the, 79–80

Fifield, A.C., 84, 100, 103

Flavell, John, 159

Flavell, Michael, 159

Flavell, Nora (née Wixey), 159

Flavell, Peter, 159–61

Frost, Robert, 94, 129

Galsworthy, John, 151

Galvin, James, 62

Gardner, Helen, 166

Garnett, Edward, 90, 95, 168

Gay, John, 13

Gibson, Wilfrid, 92, 94

Glasgow, 136

Glendower, Nailsworth, 144, 153

Gosse, Edmund, 93

Graves, Robert, 145

Gray, Thomas, 24

Great Lakes, North America, 54

Great Russell Street, 103–18

Gregynog Press, 153

Guildford, 74

Gurney, Ivor, 139

Haines, John, 139

Hamnett, Nina, 106, 157

Hardy, Thomas, 167

Harlow, Sylvia, 85

Harrison, R.U., 144

Harry Ransom Humanities Research
Center, Austin, Texas, 168

Harvey, F.W., 139

Hill, Joseph, 29

Hockey, Lawrence, 24–5, 28

Hodgson, Ralph, 102, 119, 128, 130

Hudson, W.H., 91, 118–19

Illinois, 45

Ingpen, Roger, 130

Irving, Sir Henry (John Henry
Brodribb), 20, 156